RIGHT
TO
DIE?

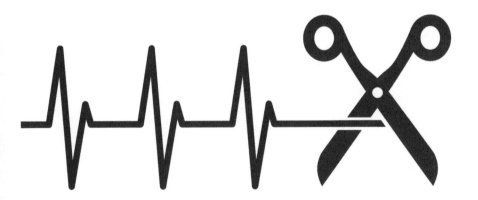

Recognizing the uncomfortable feelings of frailty, fear and vulnerability that discussions of assisted suicide and euthanasia often raise, Professor Wyatt thoughtfully navigates this highly sensitive, emotive and complex issue.

Through his assessment of the historical context, current political debate and euthanasia practices in other countries, Professor Wyatt provides a helpful resource with which to understand this issue within the Christian narrative of upholding, protecting and cherishing the inherent value and dignity of every individual.
Amelia Abplanalp, Public Policy Officer, Evangelical Alliance

The best I've read on the subject – clear, concise, compassionate. I loved it!
Lyndon Bowring, Executive Chairman, Care

This is a critical book for a critical time. John Wyatt reaches a clear, biblically based reply to those pushing the case for assisted dying. It is comprehensive, insightful and easy to follow, and essential reading for all engaged in the end-of-life debate.
Ruth Coffey, lecturer in pastoral care at Moorlands College, and formerly a nurse in a variety of settings, including hospice care

I have been campaigning against euthanasia and assisted suicide, and for more and better palliative care, for over twenty-five years now. In that time I have longed for a concise book specifically for Christians. Here it is. As parliamentary pressure continues, and many are swayed by the media, *Right to Die?* remains true to the Bible, while making an overwhelming case that is both evidence- and ethics-based.
Dr Andrew Fergusson, Chair, Advisory Group, Care Not Killing Alliance

This is a cracking book that lays out all the issues in the assisted-suicide debate compassionately and with crystal clarity. It's a road map showing the source of the euthanasia movement and the desire for control and choice that drives campaigners, and the disturbing outcomes in countries where it is already law. It warns of dangerous pressures on the elderly and disabled, and describes the 'good death' with palliative care.
Louise Morse, Christian psychotherapist, author of books on dementia (Monarch at Lion Hudson), and Media and Communications Manager for the Pilgrims' Friend Society

John Wyatt is one of those rare doctors who reflect ethically and theologically on their medical practice. With characteristic empathy, sensitivity and intellectual rigour, he dissects the popular but specious arguments in favour of assisted suicide, and issues a bold summons to the medical profession to remain faithful to its vocation of alleviating suffering rather than killing patients.
Vinoth Ramachandra, Secretary for Dialogue and Social Engagement, International Fellowship of Evangelical Students (IFES)

Why not help the terminally ill to end their miserable lives? Euthanasia and assisted suicide are the major moral issues of the day, but they have a murky past – as this brilliant book by Professor Wyatt shows. He explodes the popular myths behind the campaign for assisted dying and proposes a better way. Every caring Christian should read this. It's a matter of life and death.
Michael Wenham, author of My Donkey Body: Living with a Body That No Longer Obeys You

RIGHT TO DIE?

Euthanasia, assisted suicide and end-of-life care

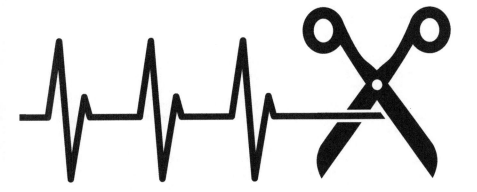

John Wyatt

Author of *Matters of Life & Death*

INTER-VARSITY PRESS
Norton Street, Nottingham NG7 3HR, England
Email: ivp@ivpbooks.com
Website: www.ivpbooks.com

British Library Cataloguing in Publication Data
A catalogue record for this book is available from the British Library.

ISBN: 978–1–78359–386–6

Set in Dante 12/15pt
Typeset in Great Britain by CRB Associates, Potterhanworth, Lincolnshire
Printed in Great Britain by Ashford Colour Press Ltd, Gosport, Hampshire

*Inter-Varsity Press publishes Christian books that are true to the Bible and that
communicate the gospel, develop discipleship and strengthen the church for its mission
in the world.*

*Inter-Varsity Press is closely linked with the Universities and Colleges Christian
Fellowship, a student movement connecting Christian Unions in universities and colleges
throughout Great Britain, and a member movement of the International Fellowship of
Evangelical Students. Website: www.uccf.org.uk*

Contents

Acknowledgments

I would like to acknowledge my gratitude to the many people who have supported and contributed to the writing of this book. To my wife Celia, who has patiently encouraged, supported and cajoled me over many months of slow progress. To my parents-in-law Malcolm and Anne Richard, who provided hospitality and support during the writing process. To my children and their spouses – JJ and Emma, Tim and Jess, Andrew and Beka – for their love, encouragement and trenchant criticism. To many friends and colleagues who have contributed to my thinking and writing about these topics, including David Jones, Peter Saunders, Rob George, Andrew Fergusson, Brian Brock, Vinoth Ramachandra, David Katz, Andrzej Turkanik, Joshua and Claire Hordern, Kate Halkerston, Kathryn Myers, Helen Barrett, David Randall, Cheryl Chin, Rick Thomas, Philippa Taylor and the members of the Christian Medical Fellowship Study Group. A special thanks to the members of an informal advisory group, Robert Wilcox, Jenny Brown, James Tomlinson, and Steve and Dot Beck.

Finally, I am indebted to Eleanor Trotter of Inter-Varsity Press, for her patience and encouragement over many delays, and for her invaluable advice and editorial guidance, and to the readers who provided feedback on an earlier draft of the manuscript. Of course, I retain responsibility for any errors and inaccuracies that remain.

Introduction

Death and dying are not comfortable topics for discussion. They raise uneasy questions and anxieties, reminding us of our own frailty and vulnerability, and opening up fears about the impending loss of our loved ones.

I have found writing this book emotionally challenging and at times disturbing. But I am absolutely convinced that these are vital topics that we cannot avoid, but must face head-on.

Just as we can't escape being confronted with death and dying in our personal lives, so also in the public arena these topics have taken on a strategic importance. Scarcely a week goes by without another high-profile media story highlighting the inadequacies of end-of-life care in our health services, or the tragic story of an individual who committed suicide to escape the suffering and indignity of a terminal illness. Some of those real-life stories feature in the subsequent chapters.

Sophisticated campaigning organizations across the world are using these personal tragedies as the driving force to change the law to allow various forms of medical killing. Their efforts seem to have been highly effective in influencing public opinion in favour of legislation for medically assisted suicide. In the UK, assisted suicide has been the topic of repeated high-profile debates in Parliament, and some have concluded that the pressure for a change in the law has become irresistible. Several prominent Christian leaders, including the previous Archbishop of Canterbury Lord Carey and South African Archbishop Desmond Tutu, have publicly stated that they have changed their minds. They are arguing that we have a specifically Christian duty to provide the option of a quick and painless suicide for those who request it at the end of life.

So what are the forces that are driving this demand for a change in the law? Is it about individual choice and control over our lives – what philosophers refer to as 'autonomy'? Or is it about the prevention of suffering? Should medical killing be restricted only to those with terminal illness, or to all who are facing hopeless and unbearable suffering? Is it possible to construct a law which has an internal logical consistency and is at the same time robust and safe in practice?

Of course, these are much more than philosophical, political or legal issues. We must never forget the personal tragedies and fears that lie behind the public debates. If we are followers of Christ, then it is our first responsibility to empathize, to try to comprehend and enter into the human suffering, fear and desperation that many people face at the end of life. We should talk about these issues not with con-demnation, judgment and rhetoric in our voices, but with tears in our eyes.

This is not an easy topic, and the public debate is often emotive, confused and confusing. I have tried to make this book as up to date as possible, but the target is continually moving, and, to my frustration as an author, fresh develop-ments are occurring almost weekly. What follows is intended for lay people and does not presume any medical knowledge. A glossary of medical and technical terms is provided at the end.

My aim in this short book is to provide a road map to the current public debate about assisted suicide and euthanasia, both in the UK and in the wider international scene. In chapters 1–3 we will look at the strange history of mercy killing, and then at current euthanasia and assisted suicide practice in countries that allow various forms of medical killing: the Netherlands, Belgium and Switzerland, and in several US states.

In chapter 4 we will look at some of the underlying social, demographic and economic forces and trends behind the pressure to change the law. In chapters 5 and 6 we will focus particularly on the two main arguments put forward in favour of medical killing: the argument from *compassion* and the argument from *autonomy* – the right to direct one's own life. Next, in chapter 7, we turn to the perspective of the historic Christian faith, and the understanding that each human life is uniquely valuable, yet fragile and dependent on others. In chapters 8 and 9 we will turn to practical medical alternatives to assisted suicide, especially to the development of modern palliative care as an effective and compassionate way of helping people to die well and 'to live before they die'.

We will also look at practical aspects of the care of the dying, including treatment decisions, advance statements or 'living wills', and the option to appoint an individual with legal powers to make medical decisions on our behalf.

In the final chapter we will look briefly at a Christian under-standing of what it means to die well and to die faithfully in the light of the Christian hope. The truth is that dying need not be an entirely negative experience. As many who have gone before us have found, the end of our lives on this earth may turn out to be a strange and wonderful opportunity for growth and internal healing, even an unexpected and unlooked-for adventure.

Writing this book has not been an easy experience. Yet I have finished with a greater confidence in the abiding relevance of historic Christian thinking to what it means to die well in the twenty-first century, and a thankfulness for the remarkable advances that have been achieved in the medical and practical care of people at the end of life. Thank you for accompanying me on this strange, uncomfortable, and yet ultimately hopeful, journey.

1870	Publication of Samuel Williams's essay on euthanasia in UK
1901	Dr Charles Goddard publishes paper on 'Suggestions in Favour of Terminating Absolutely Hopeless Cases of Injury or Disease' in UK
1922	Binding and Hoche publish *Permission for the Destruction of Worthless Life* in Germany
1935	Voluntary Euthanasia Legalisation Society founded in England
1939	Official euthanasia programme starts in Germany
1949	Dr Leo Alexander publishes paper on Nuremberg War Trials
1973	Netherlands Association for Voluntary Euthanasia (NVVE) formed
1983	First acquittal of a doctor accused of mercy killing in the Netherlands
1988	Dignitas clinic for assisted suicide opens in Zurich, Switzerland
1991	Remmelink Commission publishes results – about 1.7% of all deaths in the Netherlands due to euthanasia
	First reported case of euthanasia for psychiatric disease in the Netherlands
1994	UK Parliamentary Committee report decides against legalization of euthanasia
1997	Death with Dignity Act becomes law in the state of Oregon, USA
2002	The Netherlands formally legalizes euthanasia and medically assisted suicide
	Belgium legalizes euthanasia and medically assisted suicide
2005	Groningen Protocol on neonatal euthanasia published
2006	Assisted Dying Bill defeated in House of Lords in UK
	Voluntary Euthanasia Society in UK changes name to 'Dignity in Dying'
2008	Assisted suicide legalized in Washington State, USA
2009	Paper published on organ donation following euthanasia in Belgium
2012	NVVE creates mobile End of Life clinic in Netherlands
2014	Belgium legalizes euthanasia in children
	Falconer Assisted Dying Bill debated in House of Lords in UK
2015	Canadian Supreme Court votes in favour of medically assisted suicide
	End-of-Life Assistance Bill defeated in Scotland
	Assisted Dying Bill defeated in House of Commons in UK

Recent cases and media debates

There will be a population of demented very old people,
like an invasion of terrible immigrants, stinking out the
restaurants and cafés and shops. I can imagine a sort of civil
war between the old and the young in 10 or 15 years' time . . .
There should be a way out for rational people who have
decided they are in the negative. That should be available and
it should be easy . . . There should be a booth on every corner
where you could get a martini and a medal.

The words were mocking, cynical, deliberately provocative,
but Martin Amis was deadly serious. He had seen the protracted death of loved ones at close quarters, and he didn't
want to go in the same way.

Martin Amis is just one of a chorus of celebrities, commentators, philosophers, distinguished doctors and others,
calling for the legalization of medically assisted suicide. In
this chapter we will look at some of the prominent cases that
have influenced the current debates, including a small but
highly publicized stream of despairing suicides who make the

journey to end their lives at the Dignitas clinic in Zurich, Switzerland.

Recent cases

Edward and Joan Downes

The conductor Sir Edward Downes died at the Dignitas clinic, together with his wife Joan, a former ballerina. She had received a diagnosis of terminal liver and pancreatic cancer; he was elderly and frail, but there was no evidence of a terminal illness. They travelled to Zurich, where they were helped to commit suicide, the arrangements having been made for a fee of reportedly about £5,000 each. 'After 54 happy years together, they decided to end their own lives rather than continue to struggle with serious health problems,' reported their son Caractacus in a statement released to the press. 'They drank a small quantity of clear liquid and then lay down on the beds next to each other . . . They wanted to be next to each other when they died. It is a very civilized way to end your life, and I don't understand why the legal position in this country doesn't allow it.'

Although a person who 'aids, abets, counsels or procures the suicide of another' commits a serious criminal offence in the UK, the then Director of Public Prosecution, Keir Starmer, said that it would not be in the public interest to prosecute Caractacus Downes. This was despite evidence that he had booked the couple a hotel room in Switzerland and accompanied them on their final journey, and that he stood to gain financially from their deaths. Mr Starmer stated that

> the available evidence indicates that Mr Downes' parents had reached a voluntary, clear, settled and informed decision to take their own lives, and in assisting them, Mr Downes was

wholly motivated by compassion . . . Although his parents' wills show that Mr Downes stood to gain substantial benefit upon the death of his parents, there is no evidence to indicate that he was motivated by this prospect.

Daniel James

Another case which caused great public sympathy was that of Daniel James, a promising young rugby player for the England youth squad. In 2007, at the age of twenty-two, he suffered a spinal cord injury while playing and was permanently paralysed from the chest downwards. Daniel made an attempt on his life by swallowing an overdose while in the spinal injuries unit at Stoke Mandeville Hospital in October 2007, seven months after his injury. Six weeks later he was discharged home and took a second overdose in January 2008.

On that occasion he was taken to hospital, where a psychiatrist noted he was 'very angry and extremely hopeless'. He was also despondent that he had once again failed in his suicide bid. He refused any medical treatment, but two days later was 'calm, rational and co-operative'. He still maintained that he wanted to die, and if he did not do so from his physical problems, he would continue to attempt suicide.

His parents, who up until then had done everything they could to dissuade him, told the psychiatrist they had come to accept his wish to die. They had bought thousands of pounds' worth of equipment for their home to help with his rehabilitation, but he had shown no interest in using it. In March 2008 Daniel applied to go to Dignitas, telling his mother that if he were rejected, he intended to move out of the family home into assisted accommodation and starve himself, as 'that was the only means of ending his life in a way that he was able to control'.

In September 2008, accompanied by his parents, he travelled to Dignitas where he took a lethal dose of barbiturates. His parents were quoted as saying,

> His death was no doubt a welcome relief from the 'prison' he felt his body had become and the day-to-day fear and loathing of his living existence . . . This is the last way that the family wanted Dan's life to end, but he was, as those who know him are aware, an intelligent, strong-willed and some say determined young man.

The distinguished philosopher Baroness Mary Warnock, writing in the *Observer* newspaper, supported Daniel's parents' decision:

> They decided to believe him when he said, after he was paralysed in a scrum, that his life was of no value to him, and that he would prefer death. It was not a sudden decision, but one taken over many months, during which he had shown, by attempting suicide, that he was in deadly earnest. They made a deliberate moral choice, and carried it out in what must have been an agonising journey to Switzerland. Their courage has been enormous . . .

The number of British people who travel to Switzerland to commit suicide is tiny – between twenty and thirty a year, compared with approximately 500,000 deaths a year in the UK. But to many they represent the tip of an iceberg – the clearest manifestation of profound changes that are occurring in attitudes towards suicide and medical killing.

Tony Nicklinson

Tony Nicklinson was fifty-one when, on a business trip to Athens, a stroke left him paralysed from the neck down. The nature of the stroke led to 'locked-in syndrome', a rare condition in which conscious awareness and intelligence are unaffected, but the patient is almost totally paralysed. Tony was able to communicate only by interacting with a computer through blinking and moving his head. Nicklinson, who had lived an active life before his stroke, playing sport and travelling around the world, found it unbearable to have to be washed, dressed and fed by carers, and moved from bed to wheelchair by means of a sling. He described his life as 'dull, miserable, demeaning, undignified and intolerable'.

After the stroke he was left dependent on round-the-clock care:

> I cannot scratch if I itch. I cannot pick my nose if it is blocked, and I can only eat if I am fed like a baby – only I won't grow out of it, unlike a baby. I have no privacy or dignity left. I am washed, dressed and put to bed by carers who are, after all, still strangers. I am fed up with my life and don't want to spend the next 20 years or so like this.

It is estimated that at any one time there are up to 100 people in the UK with locked-in syndrome, yet the majority do not wish to die. They are clinging on to life, like the French editor Jean-Dominique Bauby, who gave a moving first-hand account of the experience of locked-in syndrome in his autobiography and subsequent film *The Diving Bell and the Butterfly*.

But Tony Nicklinson's insistence on his human right to die (in reality, his right to be killed by a doctor) touched a nerve with the public and media. He took his case to the Ministry of Justice, arguing that when he decided he wanted to die, the doctors who killed him should be immune from prosecution. He stated that he wanted to establish the right to die with dignity at a time of his choosing.

After protracted legal argument, the case failed. The judges described Tony's plight as 'deeply moving', demanding the most careful and sympathetic consideration. However, it was not for the High Court to decide whether the law about assisted dying should be changed and, if so, what safeguards should be put in place. 'Under our system of government these are matters for Parliament to decide, representing society as a whole, after Parliamentary scrutiny, and not for the court on the facts of an individual case or cases.' Following the verdict, Nicklinson described himself as 'devastated'. He started refusing food and deteriorated rapidly, dying from natural causes just six days after the court judgment.

Changing debates

It is striking how in the UK the public and media debate about euthanasia and assisted suicide has changed in the last twenty years. In the 1990s the debate was primarily about people who were dying in terrible and uncontrolled pain. The media was full of tragic stories of painful death. 'You wouldn't let a dog die in agony, so why do we let human beings die in this way?' And it was death from cancer which was seen as the principal problem that had to be faced. But the debate has changed. Now it is not primarily about physical pain – it has become widely accepted by most people that, with expert palliative care, pain can be reduced and controlled, if not completely eliminated. Now the main issues are *choice* and *control*. And the diseases in focus are not cancer – they are neurological diseases, such as motor neurone disease, stroke and multiple sclerosis, which cause loss of control, and dependence on others. These issues – choice, control and the fear of dependence – are now central to the debate, as we will see in subsequent chapters.

Rational suicide

The obituary of Nan Maitland, the founder of a network for social housing, is another indication of an ongoing shift in social attitudes to suicide. At first glance it was unremarkable: 'Nan Maitland died on 1 March. Her vision, energy and inspiration will be missed by all of us around the world who were captured by her warm personality and compelling charm.'

But after her death all her friends and colleagues received a letter:

> By the time you read this, with the help of Friends At The End (FATE) and the good Swiss, I will have gone to sleep, never to wake. For some time, my life has consisted of more pain than pleasure and over the next months and years the pain will be more and the pleasure less. I have a great feeling of relief that I will have no further need to struggle through each day in dread of what further horrors may lie in wait. For many years, I have feared the long period of decline, sometimes called 'prolonged dwindling', that so many people unfortunately experience before they die. Please be happy for me that I have been able to escape from this, for me, unbearable future. I have had a wonderful life, and the great good fortune to die at a time of my choosing, and in the good company of two FATE colleagues. With my death, on March 1st, I feel I am fully accepting the concept of 'old-age-rational suicide' which I have been very pleased to promote, as a founder member of the Society for Old Age Rational Suicide in the past fifteen months.

Nan Maitland's death represents a trend which is slowly growing in several countries. In the Netherlands a 2010 citizens' initiative called 'Out of Free Will' demanded that all Dutch people over seventy who feel 'tired of life' (sometimes described as having a 'completed life') should have the right to professional help in ending it. A number of prominent Dutch citizens supported the initiative, including former ministers and artists, legal scholars and physicians.

Some euthanasia activists, including the Dignitas founder Ludwig Minelli, believe in death on demand. Minelli argues that autonomy is a human right that overrides all others: 'If you accept the idea of personal autonomy, you can't make conditions that only terminally ill people should have this right.' Minelli highlights a deep division in the fundamental logic behind end-of-life legislation. Is it about autonomy and choice? Or is it about the prevention of suffering? Should assisted dying be restricted only to those with terminal illness? And is it possible to construct a law which has an internal logical consistency? These are issues to which we will return later in the book.

Human pain

These are much more than philosophical, legal or sociological issues. The brief stories above remind us of the personal tragedies and fears that lie behind the public debates. As so often, the ethical dilemmas start with human pain. With human beings who suffer and worry and weep and agonize over what will happen to them and to their loved ones. So we must never reduce these painful realities to cold philosophical or theological analysis. We are called to enter into the pain and despair of those who see no way out except suicide.

And of course the fears and anxieties raised by death and dying are not just issues 'out there' in society. They touch us all. In our darkest moments many of us have unspoken fears about what the process of dying might involve for us and for our loved ones. The prospect of an 'easy way out', a quick and painless death under our own control, may seem appealing, compassionate and humane.

Some, like Lord Carey (whom we met earlier), are arguing that we have a duty of Christian love to provide the option of a quick and painless suicide for those suffering at the end of life. Could this be an authentically Christian response? Later on I will argue that authentic Christ-like compassion leads not to medical killing and the accelerated destruction of life, but to practical caring – skilled, painstaking, costly and life-affirming.

But before that we must step back and look at the strange and murky history of mercy killing.

2

History of euthanasia and international scene

> If you don't know where you are going, it's sometimes helpful
> to know where you have been . . .
> (William Temple)

There is a strong tendency in current debates about medical killing to ignore the historical perspective. The implication is that this is a new problem which requires new solutions. Yet the reality is that euthanasia has been actively discussed in the UK for almost 150 years, while the morality of suicide and mercy killing has been a matter of debate from the pre-Christian era.

This chapter provides a brief review of the history of euthanasia both in the UK and internationally. The content that follows is therefore somewhat academic. It is also disturbing. For those who wish to fast-forward to the present and come back to this later, chapter 3 focuses on recent developments in the UK. The precise definitions of 'euthanasia' and 'assisted suicide' in the current debate are critically important, and these are discussed in that chapter.

Early developments in the UK

In 1870 an English schoolteacher, Samuel Williams, published an essay entitled 'Euthanasia'. He proposed that:

> In all cases of hopeless and painful illness, it should be the recognised duty of the medical attendant, whenever so desired by the patient, to administer chloroform, or such other anaesthetic as may by and by supersede chloroform, so as to destroy consciousness at once, and put the sufferer to a quick and painless death; all needful precautions being adopted to prevent any possible abuse of such duty, and means taken to establish, beyond the possibility of doubt or question, that the remedy was applied at the express wish of the patient.

His essay was reprinted several times and contributed to a vigorous debate on the topic.

It is striking that right from the beginning mercy killing carried out by a doctor was christened with a euphemistic title, for euthanasia means simply 'good death': *eu-thanatos*. As we will see, the use of ambiguous and misleading terminology by campaigners has been a feature of the debate right up to the current time.

There seems little doubt that the remarkable advances in medical anaesthesia in the nineteenth century had stimulated Williams's essay. Chloroform was a new, powerful (and potentially lethal) addition to medical practice, and was being used increasingly to abolish pain during childbirth and in surgical operations. Why should it not be used, under strict guidelines, to induce a painless death in cases of hopeless and painful illness? An editorial in *The Spectator* conceded that Williams's argument was persuasive, but rejected it on practical and religious grounds: 'Euthanasia would place an intolerable responsibility upon the patient, his physician and friends.'

Williams's essay was also clearly influenced by recent evolutionary thought, encapsulated in the publication of Charles Darwin's *The Origin of Species* eleven years earlier in 1859. Williams wrote,

> A universal struggle for mastery and the universal preying on the weak by the strong is incessant; where conflict, cruelties, suffering and death are in full activity at every moment in every place . . . And the only factor in all this scene of carnage that can be pointed to as significant of beneficent design, is the continuous victory of the strong, the continuous crushing out of the weak, and the consequent maintenance of what is called 'the vigour of the race', the preservation of the hardiest races and of the hardiest individuals.

Williams argued that humans already behaved in counter-evolutionary ways. Modern medicine, although commendable, effectively sponsored the survival of the 'unfit'. If this was ethically justifiable, then human beings were similarly justified in preventing the suffering which nature saw fit to impose at the end of life.

Five years later the prominent birth-control campaigner and socialist Annie Besant promoted the concept of 'rational suicide' (which we saw in the last chapter):

> . . . when we have given all we can, when strength is sinking, and life is failing, when pain wracks our bodies, and the worst agony of seeing our dear ones suffer in our anguish tortures our enfeebled minds, when the only service we can render man is to relieve him of a useless and injurious burden . . . we ask that we may be permitted to die voluntarily and painlessly,

and so to crown a noble life with the laurel wreath of a self-sacrificing death.

Radical new ideas deriving from the Enlightenment were common among elite educated thinkers in Victorian Britain. There was the potent dream of building a better future for humanity based not on religious dogma, but on science and rationality alone. At the same time the new rational philosophy of utilitarianism highlighted the moral imperative of minimizing painful and negative experiences for humans and animals alike.

Several historians have pointed to the connection between the rise of interest in euthanasia and the development of eugenics in Victorian Britain. The new 'scientific' eugenics sought to prevent racial degeneration by restricting the reproduction of those who were called the 'unfit', those with identifiable hereditary abnormalities who 'cluster to the extreme left of the distribution curve, and whose powers of reason and memory were even below those of dogs and other intelligent animals'.

In 1901 Dr Charles Goddard, a prominent supporter of both eugenics and voluntary euthanasia, and Medical Officer of Health in London, delivered a medical paper entitled 'Suggestions in Favour of Terminating Absolutely Hopeless Cases of Injury or Disease'. In it he proposed offering euthanasia both to 'those poor creatures with inaccessible and therefore inoperable malignancy', but also to mental defectives, referring to the large number of impaired individuals resident in the asylums, 'for example, idiots, beings having only semblance to human form, incapable of improvement in education, and unable to feed themselves or perceiving when the natural functions are performed, unable to enjoy life or of serving any useful purpose in nature'.

Dr Goddard's views were extreme, and were not supported by many in the overwhelmingly conservative medical profession. However, proposals for 'eugenic euthanasia' continued to be raised from time to time. Even George Bernard Shaw, in a speech to the Eugenics Education Society in 1910, was reported to have supported 'the lethal chamber' for those who wasted other people's time because they needed looking after.

The eminent neurologist Dr Tredgold was a leading authority on mental deficiency. In his textbook of 1922 he discussed the idea of a lethal chamber for those with severe mental defect. He suggested that society would 'not necessarily be unjustified' in adopting mercy killing as 'a self-defence mechanism for ridding itself of its antisocial constituents', but public opinion was such that this proposal could not be contemplated at the present juncture. Professor Richard Berry was another eminent expert in the field of mental deficiency. In 1930 he proposed a 'lethal chamber, under state control', designed for the 'painless extermination' of low-grade defectives. His views were opposed by many in the official eugenics movement, although it was noted in an official review that his proposals had 'provoked a rather surprising amount of support'.

Euthanasia in Nazi Germany and beyond

Professor Berry's proposals were similar to those put forward in Germany by Karl Binding, a professor of law, and Alfred Hoche, a professor of medicine. Their book *Permission for the Destruction of Worthless Life, Its Extent and Form*, published in 1922, identified three categories of individual in whom euthanasia or 'allowable killing' would be justified. The first consisted of patients who were terminally ill. The second included those patients who had lost consciousness and consequently were unable to make their own decision about life or death. In such cases it was proposed to have a neutral adjudicator who could anticipate their wishes for them. The third category were those described as 'incurable idiots', individuals who did not have the 'slightest use' to society and provided an enormous burden, absorbing resources which might be employed more usefully in the task of national regeneration.

The right to live, the professors asserted, must be earned and justified, not dogmatically assumed. Those who are not capable of human feelings – those 'ballast lives' and 'empty human husks' that fill our psychiatric institutions – can have no sense of the value of life. Theirs is not a life worthy of life, and hence their destruction is not only tolerable, but downright humane. The arguments in favour of mercy killing were based not only on compassion towards those who were suffering from a life not worth living, but also the huge financial cost to society which these lives represented. By 1935 popular medical and racial hygiene journals carried charts depicting the costs of maintaining the sick at the expense of the healthy.

At the same time as euthanasia was being promoted in Germany, forced sterilization of the genetically unfit was being carried out under the 1933 Law for the Prevention of Hereditary Diseased Offspring. All doctors in Germany were required to report patients of theirs who were mentally retarded, psychiatrically unwell, epileptic, blind, deaf or physically deformed. By the end of the Second World War it is estimated that over 400,000 individuals had been sterilized for eugenic reasons.

But it's important to recognize that the discussion about eugenics and euthanasia for severely impaired individuals was not restricted to Germany alone. These issues were a matter of debate in many Western countries, including the United Kingdom, the United States and Scandinavia. However, of the three categories proposed by Binding and Hoche – the terminally ill, the unconscious and the permanently disabled – it was the first category, the terminally ill who wished to be put out of their misery, that became the focus of euthanasia debate in the West. Eugenic sterilization rather than euthanasia seemed a better alternative to the problem of 'racial degeneration'.

In 1936 the Voluntary Euthanasia Society was founded in England. A Bill was submitted to Parliament, but it was defeated in the House of Lords. In opinion polls over 60% of the public supported the legalization of euthanasia. In 1937 a questionnaire among American physicians found that 53% supported euthanasia. Approximately 2,000 physicians and more than fifty religious ministers were among the members of the American Euthanasia Society in the pre-war period.

In October 1939, shortly after the outbreak of war, Hitler signed a 'euthanasia decree' authorizing specific physicians to undertake euthanasia 'so that patients who, according to human judgment, are considered incurable, can, upon a most careful diagnosis of their condition, be accorded a mercy death'. Aktion T4 was the name of the official Nazi euthanasia programme. The name T4 was derived from the address of a Berlin villa which was the headquarters of the programme, officially entitled 'Charitable Foundation for Curative and Institutional Care'. This body operated under the direction of Dr Karl Brandt, Hitler's personal physician.

A chilling film *Ich Klage An* (I accuse) was commissioned by Goebbels, at the suggestion of Karl Brandt, to make the public more supportive of the Reich's T4 euthanasia programme. A woman suffering from multiple sclerosis pleads with doctors to kill her. Her husband gives her a fatal overdose, and is put on trial. He argues that prolonging life is sometimes contrary to nature, and that death is a right as well as a duty. The film culminates with the husband's accusation of society's cruelty for trying to prevent such deaths. This sentimental and misleading portrait of euthanasia was of course far from the terrible realities of the T4 programme.

The official T4 statistics recorded that 70,273 people were killed, but in 1946 the Nuremberg War Trials found evidence that in reality about 275,000 people were killed under T4. The programme included newborns and very young children. Midwives and doctors were required to report to T4 officials those children up to the age of three who showed signs of mental retardation, physical deformity or other symptoms.

In 1949 an American psychiatrist, Leo Alexander, who had attended the Nuremberg War Trials, wrote an influential paper entitled 'Medical Science under Dictatorship', published in the *New England Journal of Medicine*. In it he traced the historical roots of the Nazi euthanasia movement. How was it that respected doctors could have participated in such horrendous acts? Alexander concluded,

It started with the acceptance by doctors of the idea, basic in the euthanasia movement, that there is such a thing as a life not worthy to be lived. This attitude in the beginning referred to the severely and chronically sick. Gradually the sphere of those to be included was enlarged to encompass the socially unproductive, the ideologically unwanted, the racially unwanted . . . But it is important to realise that the infinitely small lever from which this entire trend of mind received its impetus was the attitude towards the incurably sick.

'The life not worthy to be lived'. This idea was the 'infinitely small lever' that led inexorably to the catastrophic consequences of the T4 euthanasia programme. Leo Alexander's conclusion seems remarkably prescient. As we will see, this idea is still around, and it is central to the current push for euthanasia and assisted suicide. When, as legislation that is being debated in many countries might allow, I agree to assist your suicide, I am in effect agreeing with you that your life is not worth living. What would be the long-term consequences in our society of this 'infinitely small lever'?

The idea of the life not worthy to be lived was the 'infinitely small lever' that led to euthanasia.

As the unspeakable horrors of the Nazi euthanasia programme emerged into public view after the end of the Second World War, it is not surprising that the demand for the legalization of euthanasia in the rest of Europe subsided for a period.

Euthanasia in the Netherlands

We will examine the development and current practice of euthanasia in the Netherlands in some detail, not least because it provides an instructive example of how various forms of mercy killing have become increasingly acceptable within a modern European context over a forty-year period, together with the challenges this has posed for doctors.

Attitudes towards euthanasia and the process of dying started changing in the Netherlands in the 1970s. Commentators have suggested that this reflected both changes in cultural attitudes and changes in medical technology. On the cultural front there was increasing individualism, secularism and a desire for democratic discussion and debate about death and dying. At the same time there was a new awareness of the impact of new medical technology, increasing doctors' ability to postpone death.

Questions about the prolongation and the termination of life became the subject of public debate. TV shows and radio programmes investigated the process of dying and the importance of being told the truth at one's deathbed. Symposia were organized, and 'support in the dying process' became a familiar concept. Opinion polls showed that a growing proportion of the population thought that life could sometimes be actively terminated and that 'euthanasia' should be made legal.

To begin with, the word 'euthanasia' was used with a range of meanings, but a process of conceptual clarification gradually took place. Over time the word came to refer exclusively to the active termination of life, usually by a doctor administering a lethal injection. This was distinguished from the withdrawal of life-supporting treatment and the use of pain-controlling medication at the end of life, which came to be regarded as 'normal medical practice'. 'Euthanasia' in the Netherlands today is almost universally defined as the situation in which a doctor kills a person who is suffering 'unbearably' and 'hopelessly', at the latter's explicit request.

In 1973 the Netherlands Association for Voluntary Euthanasia (NVVE) was formed. It remains active and influential to this present day. The Association's stated goal was to work towards the social acceptance and the legalization of voluntary euthanasia. To distinguish its aims from the horrors of the Nazi euthanasia programme, the NVVE has always emphasized that euthanasia should be entirely voluntary in nature. One of its most important roles has been the formulation and distribution of 'euthanasia statements' or advance directives, in which a person declares that, should an illness or accident 'cause such physical or mental damage that recuperation to a reasonable and dignified standard of life becomes impossible', he or she refuses all curative treatment and wishes to have euthanasia performed.

Until 2002 euthanasia was explicitly prohibited by the Dutch Criminal Code. But from the 1980s, the Dutch courts have held that a defence of 'necessity' was available to a doctor charged with intentional homicide or assisted suicide. The first acquittal of a doctor accused of mercy killing took place in 1983, and this was upheld by the Dutch Supreme Court. The essence of the legal defence was that the doctor was confronted by an irreconcilable conflict. On the one hand there was an absolute medical duty to prevent suffering which was 'unbearable and hopeless'. On the other hand there was a medical duty to protect and preserve life. Faced with this intractable conflict of duties, the doctor could claim that he or she had no choice but to terminate the patient's life as the only means to bring an end to the suffering.

During the 1980s a series of test cases developed the procedures by which a doctor who had terminated the life of a patient could claim immunity from prosecution. The doctor had to demonstrate that he or she had acted 'with due care'. Over time this was specified as:

1. The request for euthanasia must be voluntary and uncoerced.
2. The request must be 'well-considered' (in other words, rationally defensible).
3. The patient's desire to die must be a lasting one.
4. The patient must experience their suffering as unacceptable or 'unbearable'. It was the doctor's task to investigate whether there were medical or social interventions that might make the patient's suffering bearable.

5. The doctor concerned must consult an experienced colleague.

It is important to note, first, the emphasis on 'unbearable and hopeless suffering'. In order for euthanasia to be legally justified in the Netherlands, there has to be suffering which is both 'unbearable', that is, experienced by the patient as totally unacceptable and intolerable, and 'hopeless', that is, there is no possibility of amelioration through medical treatment or social intervention. Clearly, suffering is a subjective experience which only the patient can describe, but it is the clinical responsibility of the doctor to determine whether the patient's suffering reaches the level of being both 'unbearable' and 'hopeless'. There have been many cases in the Netherlands where the patient's request for euthanasia has been turned down by his or her doctor because the degree of suffering was regarded as insufficient.

Secondly, euthanasia can only be legally performed by a physician, and within the context of an established doctor–patient relationship. Only a physician can experience an irreconcilable conflict between the medical duties to relieve suffering and to protect life.

Thirdly, there is no requirement in Dutch law and practice for the patient to have a terminal illness, or to have a purely physical source of suffering. Provided that the threshold of 'unbearable and hopeless suffering' is reached, any patient is free to request euthanasia and his or her doctor can claim the protection of legal necessity.

Fourthly, although in the Netherlands the term 'euthanasia' is only applied to the voluntary request of a legally competent patient (one in full possession of rational faculties), it is clear that the legal defence of necessity could in principle apply to *any* patient who was suffering unbearably and hopelessly.

Whether the patient was competent or not, and whether he or she was requesting euthanasia or not, the physician would still be placed in an irreconcilable conflict of duties. If a physician had a duty to end the unbearable suffering of a legally competent adult, why would there be no duty to end the life of a suffering baby, a patient in a permanent coma, or someone with advanced dementia?

In 1991 the results of the Remmelink Commission, an official investigation into the extent of euthanasia in the Netherlands, were published. About 1.7% of all deaths (2,300) per year were due to euthanasia and 0.2% (400 deaths) to assisted suicide. The research also revealed, controversially, that in about 0.8% (1,000 deaths) the life of a patient was ended without there being an explicit request.

Current euthanasia practice in the Netherlands

In 2002 the Netherlands became the first country in the world to legalize both euthanasia and medically assisted suicide. The Termination of Life on Request and Assisted Suicide (Review Procedures) Act formalized the practice which had evolved over the preceding twenty or thirty years. Currently there are about 4,000 cases of euthanasia and assisted suicide (about 3% of all deaths in the Netherlands) per year.

The commonest means of euthanasia is by lethal injection, usually with very large doses of barbiturate. Medically assisted suicide usually involves swallowing a lethal dose of barbiturates, prescribed and overseen by a doctor. In addition, many more die from the increasingly common practice of terminal or 'palliative' sedation, deliberately rendering a patient unconscious and withholding fluids and nutrition until death occurs. This practice does not require official reporting, but a report estimated that it accounted for about 8% of deaths in 2005, rising to about 12% in 2010. One Dutch parliamentarian, commenting on the rise in the practice of terminal sedation, said, 'Palliative sedation is easier for doctors. There is no control by the euthanasia committee, and it is emotionally easier, too.' There is further discussion of palliative sedation in Appendix 4 (page 168).

Psychiatric illness

In September 1991 Dr Boudewijn Chabot, a psychiatrist, supplied his patient, Ms B, with lethal drugs. Ms B was a fifty-year-old with a prolonged psychiatric illness which had proved resistant to treatment. She had lost all desire to go on living and had made at least one previous suicide attempt. She consumed the lethal drugs in the presence of Chabot and died shortly afterwards. Chabot reported her death as a suicide which he had assisted. He was prosecuted, and the case went ultimately to the Dutch Supreme Court. The Court concluded that unbearable suffering that was psychological in origin could provide justification for medical assistance with suicide, but it criticized Chabot for failing to ensure that his patient was examined by an independent colleague. Following the court judgment there has been a small but significant number of patients with untreatable psychiatric illness who have received euthanasia in the Netherlands.

A 2013 interview with a Dutch psychiatrist, Dr Paulan Stärcke, published on the NVVE website, illustrated the way in which professional attitudes are changing. Stärcke said that initially discussion about euthanasia in psychiatric patients was taboo, but following the 2002 euthanasia legislation, things started to change. 'According to the law, a physician can carry out euthanasia and – as an institution – we could not say no to it anymore . . .' In 2009 the first serious discussion about assisted suicide took place, following a request from a

sixty-four-year-old woman with depression and a serious com-
pulsion disorder. Early in 2010 a demented woman asked for
euthanasia. She was admitted to hospital because she was
psychotic and she could not return home. Dr Stärcke assisted
her suicide with lethal drugs. She stated that many of her
colleagues were anxious about euthanasia, so she decided to
help out. Instead of just being the coach, she took over the
euthanasia request if the psychiatrist was anxious.

In the interview Stärcke was asked whether the act of
euthanasia was not a heavy responsibility.

> As a psychiatrist you always take heavy ethical decisions:
> forcible admission, separation. These are not easy decisions.
> I find assisting in suicide an act of mercy. We do not have
> much to offer to people with chronic psychiatric disease.
> And for some patients we can do nothing. In schizophrenia,
> personality disorders and bipolar disease you can fight the
> symptoms, reduce the suffering and teach patients to live
> with it, but there is no cure available. The medicines you
> prescribe do have unpleasant side effects. If someone says to
> me, 'This is unbearable', who am I to say 'Go on, it may
> become tolerable' . . . Patients with depression or anorexia
> nervosa receive euthanasia relatively more frequently than
> other patients. In those clinical situations it is clear which
> treatment to give and whether you have taken all the steps.
> Then you can say you have tried everything. Besides, we
> know if the depression has lasted for a long time, it is very
> difficult to treat . . .

This striking interview suggests that, at least in some psychiatric institutions in the Netherlands, there has been a move
towards the acceptance of medically assisted suicide as a
'therapeutic option'. The annual number of reported cases of

euthanasia in psychiatric illness in 2013 was forty-five, a threefold rise compared with fourteen in 2012.

Extension of euthanasia to other adult conditions

Currently in the Netherlands most cases of euthanasia are in patients with cancer. This practice seems widely accepted by the population as a whole and by doctors. Fewer than 10% of doctors refuse to participate in the process on the grounds of conscience. The main focus of debate is on the availability of euthanasia for other conditions, particularly in patients with dementia, those with psychiatric conditions, and older people who feel they have a 'completed life'.

Recently, the Royal Dutch Medical Association (KNMG) published a position paper on whether euthanasia was justified in these controversial areas. The paper reflects the pressure that some physicians feel to perform euthanasia in elderly people with dementia and other chronic conditions, to conform with public expectations. (An extract from the KNMG position paper is available in Appendix 2.)

It is clear that a significant number of Dutch doctors are modifying their clinical practice in response to strong public pressure to extend euthanasia to patients with dementia and those deemed to be suffering unbearably from psychiatric illness. But the KNMG is currently resolutely opposed to the medical practice of euthanasia where the only indication is that an elderly person is 'tired of life'.

In Appendix 2 I have quoted this document in detail because it seems highly significant in describing the pressures and conflicts that many doctors experience due to the availability of legalized euthanasia and increasing pressure from patients and relatives. In fact, a major survey of 1,500 Dutch doctors published in February 2015 reported that 18% would consider 'helping someone to die' even if they had no physical problems but were 'tired of living'.

In 2012 the NVVE set up an independent End of Life clinic for patients who had requested euthanasia but whose own doctors had refused. The End of Life clinic consists of sixteen mobile teams (each consisting of a physician and a nurse) and a building in The Hague for staff and telephone co-workers. The euthanasia or assisted suicide is carried out at the home of the person requesting help. At the end of the first year, the team reported 714 requests for help, mostly from people aged between eighty-one and ninety. The total number of deaths in that period was unclear, and a significant number were said to be 'on the waiting list' for euthanasia.

Another striking trend in the Netherlands is the increasing publicity about self-help methods for people who wish to kill themselves. In 2012 a film made by the psychiatrist Dr Chabot explained how someone can kill themselves using helium. Chabot had been involved in promoting 'self-administered euthanasia', using methods such as slowly gathering together a lethal combination of medicines. However, he then released a film showing how inhaled helium can be used to ensure rapid death from hypoxia.

To mark Euthanasia Week in 2012, the NVVE organized 'The End', publicized as the first-ever film festival devoted to the subject of euthanasia. One film, *Medeleven* (Sympathy), showed a ninety-one-year-old man travelling to pharmacies in Belgium to buy drugs for a lethal dose. His wife had died and he did not want to go on living, but he failed to meet the criteria for legal euthanasia. The film showed the relief the man felt when he finally obtained the suicide drugs: he had taken control.

NVVE director Petra de Jong stated that she believed the taboo about death had diminished since the introduction of euthanasia legislation. 'The subject has become a part of life. A result of this is that people really want to be in control. I increasingly see self-help methods being discussed.'

Neonatal euthanasia

In 1995 a Dutch gynaecologist, Dr Henk Prins, was accused of the murder of a three-day-old baby with severe spina bifida. The medical team responsible, in consultation with her parents, had earlier decided to cease further medical treatment, and in particular not to operate on her spina bifida because such surgery was considered medically futile. The baby was said to be suffering unbearable pain, and the doctors and the parents decided to give her a lethal injection. The gynaecologist claimed the legal defence of 'necessity'. As a compassionate doctor, he had no choice but to put the baby out of her misery. The District Court held that active termination of life without an explicit request by the person concerned could be justifiable if certain requirements were met.

In 2005 the prestigious *New England Journal of Medicine* published the 'Groningen Protocol', a procedure for regularizing the euthanasia of newborns in the Netherlands. This protocol described three groups of infants in whom deliberate life-ending procedures could be taken: those with no chance of survival, those with a poor prognosis who are dependent on intensive care, and those with a 'hopeless prognosis who experience what parents and medical experts deem to be unbearable suffering'. The paper described twenty-two reported cases between 1997 and 2004, nearly all of which were babies with severe spina bifida.

A national survey in the Netherlands suggested that euthanasia was being carried out in fifteen to twenty newborns each year, but the number of reported cases was much lower. The publication of the Groningen Protocol aroused considerable controversy around the world, but it has received strong support from a number of medical ethicists.

Assisted suicide in Oregon

It is striking that the way in which medically assisted suicide developed in the US state of Oregon was fundamentally different from the Netherlands. In Oregon the conceptual framework is not centred on the duty of the doctor to treat unbearable suffering, but rather the right of every patient to die in a way that they themselves perceive as dignified. According to one campaigner, 'The greatest human freedom is to live, and die, according to one's own desires and beliefs.'

The Death with Dignity Act became law in the state of Oregon in 1997. This law allows a 'capable' adult patient who is a resident of Oregon, and with less than six months to live, to request a prescription for a lethal dose of drugs. The patient must take the drugs by themselves and cannot be physically assisted by the doctor. Physicians are encouraged to report cases, but the system is based entirely on trust. There is no specific regulatory authority, no resources are made available to ensure compliance with the law, and there are no penalties for doctors who fail to report assisted-suicide deaths. When concerns were raised about a patient who woke up three days after taking the supposedly lethal medication, the State Department of Human Services said it had no authority to investigate individual death-with-dignity cases.

It should be noticed that whereas 'unbearable and hopeless suffering' is an essential feature before euthanasia or assisted suicide can be considered in the Netherlands, in Oregon there is no requirement for the patient to be suffering at all.

In the official report for 2014 from Oregon the reasons given for requesting assisted suicide were as follows:

'Losing autonomy' 91%
'Less able to engage in activities making life enjoyable' 86%
'Loss of dignity' 75%
'Losing control of bodily functions' 49%
'Burden on family, friends / caregivers' 40%
'Inadequate pain control or concern about it' 31%

One Oregon doctor commented, 'They are not using assisted suicide because they need it for the usual medical kinds of reasons; they are using it because they tend to be people who have always controlled the circumstances of their lives and they prefer to control their death in the same way.'

Only 3 out of 105 patients who died by assisted suicide in 2014 had been referred for psychiatric evaluation. Since the law was passed in 1997, a total of 1,327 people have had lethal prescriptions written, and 859 patients have died from taking lethal medications prescribed under the Death with Dignity Act. A steady increase in the rate of assisted suicide has been observed over a decade, rising steadily from 16 in 1998 to 105 in 2014, but the total number remains small at approximately 3 per 1,000 deaths in Oregon.

The standard method for assisted suicide in Oregon involves the oral ingestion of a massive overdose of barbiturates. Not surprisingly, there are case reports in which the suicide attempt has been unsuccessful because of vomiting. In fact, the Oregon approach has been opposed by Dutch euthanasia specialists. 'Taking 90 barbiturate tablets is not a harmless procedure: it causes vomiting; it tastes awful; it is painful. If you are going to have a quick and easy death from some kind of euthanasia or assisted suicide, you have to have lethal injection . . .'

In Oregon any appointed person, such as a family member or a volunteer from Compassion and Choices, may pick up the lethal medication from the pharmacy and deliver it to the patient's home. The medication could then remain in the patient's home for a year or more; no safeguards are in place to ensure that it is stored safely and returned to the pharmacy if unused.

Similar legislation to that of Oregon has been passed in Washington State, New Mexico, Montana and Vermont.

In February 2015 the Canada Supreme Court ruled that Canadian provinces could not legally prohibit medically assisted suicide, provided that the patient suffered from a 'grievous and irremediable medical condition'. There was no requirement for the patient to be terminally ill.

Euthanasia in Belgium

In September 2002 an act legalizing euthanasia in Belgium came into effect. The wording was very similar to the Dutch legislation. However, the act explicitly included mental suffering as an indication for euthanasia, stating, 'the patient should be in a medically hopeless condition of constant and unbearable physical or mental suffering, which cannot be cured and which is a consequence of a severe and incurable disorder caused by accident or disease.'

A 2006 paper published in the *British Journal of Psychiatry* by a group of Belgian psychiatrists argued for the right of psychiatrists to assist the suicide of their patients. While recognizing the potential for abuse of euthanasia for psychiatric patients, they stated that paradoxically,

The main argument in favour of assistance with suicide for patients who primarily have a mental disorder arises from the area of suicide prevention. The demand for euthanasia by a patient means that life at that particular moment is unbearable to the patient and that something has to change . . . From this point of view, it is important to take this request seriously and open it up for discussion. In these circumstances a therapeutic relationship can be established in which space can be found to restore hope in the patient. When this has been sufficiently achieved, alternative treatment options may be considered by the patient.

Further arguments in favour are mainly based on compassion. Essentially, most patients suffering primarily from a mental disorder are physically capable of suicide, hence – some may argue – it is not really necessary to provide assistance. If no assistance is provided, however, the patient may be more likely to attempt suicide in lonely, difficult circumstances and in a risky and violent way. Moreover, such patients may run the risk of failing in their suicide attempt, and instead harm themselves seriously and permanently. Once the legal requirements have been met, assistance with suicide may create the opportunity for a more humane method of suicide. Furthermore, prevention of violent suicide can be seen as a measure to protect people who might become accidentally involved in, and traumatised by, the patient's suicide.

In 2014 Belgian legislation was passed which would allow euthanasia in children of any age, although parents would have a role in their decision to die. 'We want to provide freedom of choice also to minors who are able to make up their own mind,' said one of the Bill's backers. 'The legislation will give a merciful way out for young people suffering from debilitating conditions and legalise a practice that is already going on in secret.'

Assisted suicide in Switzerland

Switzerland has a unique legal approach. Assisted suicide has been legal since 1941 if performed by a non-physician without a vested interest in that individual's death. The law prohibits doctors, spouses, children or other such related parties from directly participating in the suicide of another. Hence, whereas in the Netherlands and several US states only a physician may authorize the legal suicide of another, in Switzerland a physician is prohibited from directly assisting such an act; only a lay person may directly participate in a suicide.

The Dignitas clinic in Zurich was referred to on several occasions in the case histories in the first chapter. It was set up in 1988 and, according to its website, has 'helped more than 1,700 people to end their lives gently, safely, without risk and usually in the presence of family members and/or friends'. Following medical assessment, clients are prescribed a very large dose of an oral barbiturate, together with an anti-sickness medication. Both medications are taken under the supervision of a volunteer, but a physician cannot be present. Over 80% of those who commit suicide with the help of Dignitas come from outside Switzerland, with the largest group coming from Germany, followed by the UK.

Although there has been controversy about some of Dignitas's procedures, and about the reality of 'suicide tourism' in Switzerland, the practice was supported in a referendum of the local population. The basis on which clients are assessed for suitability for suicide is not clear, and there has been controversy about clients who were obviously not terminally ill. Ludwig Minelli, the Dignitas director, agrees that some of those who receive assisted suicide are people who are just tired of life:

> If you accept the idea of personal autonomy, you can't make conditions that only terminally ill people should have this right . . . With life expectancy growing and medical sophistication improving, people are increasingly worried about whether they will be condemned to linger on, forced to end their lives in an institution. Our members say: with our pets, when they are old and in pain, we help them. Why am I not entitled to go to the vet? Why haven't I such an opportunity? We hear this often.

Minelli's vision goes beyond helping the infirm to shorten a painful end. He believes that the right to choose to die is a fundamental human one and, in theory, he is willing to help anyone. However, Swiss medical regulations prohibit doctors from assisting the suicide of healthy people, and they restrict assisted suicide for the mentally ill – making it practically impossible for Dignitas to help people who are profoundly depressed to kill themselves. This is a prohibition that Minelli is fighting.

Dignitas staff argue that once a client has been assessed as suitable for assisted suicide, the possibility is enough to

> relieve people burdened by disease and suffering because it acts as a kind of escape valve. The individual is no longer the helpless and indiscriminate victim of fate, but rather sees a new opportunity to take control of his or her own destiny. Thanks to this option, many people then decide to await their uncertain future. They do this because they know that they have the possibility later on to definitely end their lives themselves with Dignitas, should their situation become too

difficult. Along the way, they realise that they are actually stronger than they thought. In addition, suitable palliative care is often helpful in maintaining an acceptable quality of life for them.

Approximately thirty people travel from the UK to the Dignitas clinic every year for assisted suicide. But why should those people who are desperate to kill themselves be required to travel to Switzerland? Many have argued that it would be more compassionate and humane to change the law to make this practice legal in the UK. In the next chapter we will look at the history of assisted suicide legislation in the UK.

3

United Kingdom experience

As details of the Nazi euthanasia programme became well known in the years following the Second World War, it is not surprising that discussion about legalizing euthanasia in the UK died down. However, the Voluntary Euthanasia Legislation Society, which had been formed in 1935, kept up the pressure. A debate in the House of Lords in 1950 met with overwhelming opposition. However, the Society gained strong backing from Professor Glanville Williams, an eminent and influential lawyer, who supported the medical killing of patients who were enduring a miserable life, even if natural death was not imminent.

The 1961 Suicide Act removed the legal penalties for attempted suicide, although assisting remained a serious criminal offence. There was renewed discussion, although interestingly, much of the public debate at the time focused on children with severe disabilities, and the 'agonies' of parents caring for such children, sometimes to the extent of being 'forced' to take the law into their own hands by killing them. Further attempts at legalizing euthanasia failed, and in 1978 the Voluntary Euthanasia Society published a self-help booklet, *Guide to Self-Deliverance*, which provided advice about the most effective ways of committing suicide. Not surprisingly, this caused widespread controversy and debate, and the Society was increasingly seen as marginalized and extreme.

In 1994 a Select Committee of the House of Lords on Medical Ethics published a major report which concluded that although there were particular cases where euthanasia might seem appropriate, 'individual cases could not reasonably establish the foundation of a policy which would have such serious and widespread repercussions'. A group from the House of Lords had visited the Netherlands, and Dutch-style euthanasia legislation did not seem an attractive option in the UK. As we will see in a later chapter, it is clear that the development of modern palliative care in the UK, pioneered by Dame Cicely Saunders at St Christopher's Hospice in London, had a very influential role in providing an alternative to euthanasia. As Dr Saunders argued, 'You don't have to kill the patient in order to kill the pain.'

Campaigners aim for assisted suicide, not euthanasia

All recent attempts at legalization in the UK have focused on medically assisted suicide rather than euthanasia. Campaigners have concluded that assisting suicide is more acceptable to the public, in line with Anglo-Saxon preoccupations with individual choice and freedom. In public debates supporters have distanced themselves from euthanasia as practised in the Netherlands and Belgium. Instead, it is argued, proposed legislation will be limited to 'assisting the dying' of a small number of terminally ill individuals who wish to end their lives.

However, in private, many campaigners concede that proposed legislation will not satisfy the highly publicized needs of those who are very severely disabled and unable to commit suicide (such as Tony Nicklinson), nor those who wish to die but are not terminally ill (such as Daniel James). Many, such as Baroness Mary Warnock, regard the legalization of assisted suicide as the first step towards a more wide-reaching liberalization of the law to allow suicide and mercy killing in a range of circumstances.

In 2006 the distinguished human rights lawyer Lord Joffe introduced the Assisted Dying Bill in the House of Lords. Its aim was to legalize assisted suicide in England and Wales under strictly controlled circumstances, including a life expectancy of less than six months and 'unbearable suffering', defined as 'suffering, whether by reason of pain, distress or otherwise which the patient finds so severe as to be unacceptable'. The Bill was defeated by a vote in the House of Lords.

In the same year the Voluntary Euthanasia Society changed its name to 'Dignity in Dying'. The choice of words is, of course, highly significant, and symbolic of a profound change in the presentation of the arguments for a change in the law. Since then Dignity in Dying has become a highly effective lobbying organization with a number of distinguished and prominent supporters, including many well-known celebrity names.

In Scotland Margo MacDonald, a very popular member of the Scottish Parliament, introduced an End-of-Life Assistance Bill, which proposed that assisted suicide should be available to those who had 'a terminal illness or a terminal condition' and who 'find their life intolerable'. As in England, the legislation was modelled on Oregon-style assisted suicide. The Bill was defeated on several occasions in the Scottish Parliament, and despite Margo MacDonald's death in 2014 from natural causes (she had suffered from Parkinson's disease for many years), attempts at introducing similar legislation continue. In

2015 an Assisted Suicide Scotland Bill was defeated in the Scottish Parliament.

Lord Falconer's Assisted Dying Bill

In 2014 Lord (Charles) Falconer introduced another Bill for the legalization of assisted suicide in England and Wales. The criteria were similar to Lord Joffe's, except that any requirement that the individual should have 'severe and unacceptable suffering' was completely removed. The wording of the Bill was based closely on the findings of a 2012 Commission, supported by Dignity in Dying, and chaired by Lord Falconer, which stated,

> We firmly believe it is only for the individual concerned to judge the extent of the suffering caused by their illness. We are also concerned that a person who has a terminal illness should not be required to be already experiencing unbearable suffering to request an assisted death; it could be the prospect of anticipated suffering that he or she does not wish to experience that gives rise to the request for assistance.

The report of the 2012 Falconer Commission stated,

> We have taken on board the strong concerns expressed by many disabled people and do not consider that it would be acceptable to society at this point in time to recommend that a non-terminally ill person with significant physical impairments should be made eligible under any future legislation to request assistance in ending his or her life. The intention of the Commission in recommending that any future legislation should permit assisted suicide exclusively for those who are terminally ill and specifically excluding disabled people (unless

they are terminally ill) is to establish a clear delineation between the application of assisted suicide to people who are terminally ill and others with long-term conditions or impairments. This is something that the Director of Public Prosecution's policy currently fails to achieve. The adoption of this distinction in any future legislation would send a clear message to the British public that disabled people's lives are equally valued and that if the 'opportunity' does not exist the 'obligation' cannot follow in the UK.

'However,' the report continued, 'we are concerned that those who might agree to assist a non-terminally ill loved one, who has suffered such a catastrophic life-changing event, to commit suicide for wholly compassionate reasons (for example, the parents of Daniel James) should continue to be treated by the law with compassion and understanding.'

It is notable that the word 'suicide' is carefully avoided in the wording of the proposed legislation. Instead, the euphemistic and ambiguous phrase 'assisted dying' is used throughout. Yet within the body of the Bill, assistance in dying is defined as the prescription of medication by a doctor to enable a terminally ill person to end their own life. In other words, it represents a major change in the criminal law on killing and the protection of human life.

The wording of the Bill allows an assisting health professional to:

a. prepare lethal medicine for self-administration by the terminally ill person;
b. prepare a medical device which will enable that person to self-administer the medicine; and
c. assist that person to ingest or otherwise self-administer the medicine.

However, 'the decision to self-administer the medicine and the final act of doing so must be taken by the person for whom the medicine has been prescribed'.

In 2014 the Bill was debated in a highly publicized session of the House of Lords. The Bill failed to progress, but a very similar Bill was introduced into the House of Commons by MP Rob Marris in 2015. This was convincingly defeated, with 330 voting against compared with 118 in favour. Activists for assisted suicide vowed to fight on, claiming that the vote showed that Members of Parliament were 'ridiculously out of touch with the British public on the issue'.

In the next chapter we will turn to some of the social pressures that lie behind the drive for euthanasia and assisted suicide, and then in subsequent chapters, 5 and 6, we will look in greater detail at the two principal arguments put forward in Parliament in favour of a change in the law: the argument from compassion and the argument from autonomy.

However, before addressing these wider issues, it is important briefly to reflect on the language that is being used in the contemporary debate.

The language of the debate

It is striking that from the very beginning debates about euthanasia and suicide have always been bedevilled by misleading and euphemistic language, and it seems that this phenomenon is particularly common in the UK. At least the Dutch are straightforward in their discussion of euthanasia and assisting suicide. In the UK we meet euphemisms such as 'an assisted death', 'ending suffering when it becomes unbearable', 'easeful death', 'choice and control at the end of life', 'easing the passing', 'merciful relief' and 'stopping unnecessary suffering at the end of life'.

The change in title of the Voluntary Euthanasia Society into Dignity in Dying is itself highly significant. Without prior knowledge, one would naturally assume that the organization supported dying people to ensure that all their care needs were met and that their dignity was preserved. In reality, the sole aim of the organization is to campaign for the legalization of medically assisted suicide. The implication of course is that dignity in dying can only be achieved by suicide.

In the literature produced by Dignity in Dying, the word 'suicide' is assiduously avoided, presumably because of its unhelpful connotations. Instead, the euphemistic and misleading phrases 'assisted death' and 'assisted dying' are used throughout.

What does 'assisted dying' mean?

In response to the use of the phrase 'assisted dying', a senior palliative care nurse wrote,

> Midwives assist birth, and palliative care nurses assist the dying with specialist palliative care. Assistance is not the same as killing. The use of the term 'assisted dying' is offensive to those of us who are giving good care at the end of life. It is a deception to sanitize killing to make it more acceptable to the public.

In normal English use, 'dying' implies a natural process, whereas 'suicide' implies the active and deliberate termination of one's life. 'Assisted dying' sounds positive and uncontroversial. Yet it is being used to describe not the normal care and assistance of dying people, which is a major part of healthcare across the UK, but the intentional planning, preparation and direct assistance of a suicide, a serious criminal offence under the Suicide Act.

It is interesting to reflect on why those who wish to campaign for a change in the law, including many eminent lawyers whose careers have depended on the precise forensic use of language, are so reluctant to use straightforward un-ambiguous English in this case. I suggest that it indicates how important language is in the way we as human beings assess the morality of our actions. The words we use to describe our own actions and the actions of others do matter. Those who are campaigning for a change in the law are well aware that many people in our society have deep intuitive concerns about legalized killing and suicide. So if I describe my actions as 'assisting a dying person', I am more likely to conclude that it is morally acceptable, compared with 'helping someone to kill themselves'.

In the history of ethics, it often seems that the manipulation of language precedes a change in behaviour.

In the history of ethics, it often seems that the manipulation of language precedes a change in behaviour. But careful moral assessment depends on the accurate and unambiguous use of language. As an ancient proverb puts it, 'The beginning of wisdom is to call things by their proper names.'

Defining euthanasia

A widely accepted definition of euthanasia is: 'The intentional medical killing, by act or omission, of an individual whose life is thought to be not worth living'.

Note first the emphasis on *intentional killing*, a deliberate and premeditated act to take life, to introduce death into a situation. Even if a person has a terminal illness, the intention is that death should occur at a specified time using lethal drugs. The intention to kill is revealed in the choice of drugs used by doctors in the Netherlands for euthanasia. As we know, they usually employ a barbiturate in extremely high dosage, and this is coupled with an intravenous muscle-relaxant drug designed to stop respirations instantaneously. These drugs are totally different from those used in palliative care. There the intention is to use drugs that control symptoms of pain and distress, not to hasten death, and therefore only those that do not carry a risk of killing are employed. But in euthanasia different drugs are used, with one intention only – to induce death rapidly and 'cleanly'. The intention of the doctor is that the patient should die quickly and without complications. To refer to this process as 'assisted dying' is to stretch language to breaking point.

Secondly, note that according to this definition, euthanasia may be performed either positively by deliberate act, or negatively by omission. It is the intention to kill which is central to the definition. Hence, it can be argued that to use medication to put a person into a persistent coma over many days, but deliberately omit to give any form of fluid or nutrition so that the person dies eventually of dehydration, is as much a form of intentional medical killing as to inject a lethal quantity of a barbiturate.

In the past the phrases 'active euthanasia' and 'passive euthanasia' have been widely used, but most ethicists now agree that they are ambiguous and should be dropped.

Thirdly, note that euthanasia, intentional killing, is not the same as withdrawing or withholding medical treatment that can bring no benefit, or that is excessively burdensome to the patient. This is universally regarded as good medical practice, not intentional killing. (I will discuss this issue in more detail in chapter 8.)

Defining assisted suicide

Doctor-assisted suicide is practically and morally very closely related to euthanasia. Again, the intention of the doctor is that the patient should die rapidly and 'cleanly'. He or she calculates the lethal dose, usually a massive dose of an oral barbiturate, many times that normally prescribed.

The doctor ensures that the medication is available, and gives detailed instructions on how the drugs should be taken to ensure that death occurs rapidly and without complications. The patient must be instructed to remain upright after swallowing the barbiturate to reduce the risk of inhaling vomit. In cases where the patient is unable to take the drug orally, the doctor may prepare a mechanism for the drugs to be administered artificially, including inserting an intravenous line, and obtaining and drawing up the drugs into a syringe, although the patient must make the final decision by pressing a button.

Throughout this process the actions of the doctor are intended to end the life of the patient, to introduce death. He or she has agreed with the patient that their life is not worth living. But the physician hangs back from the final step – the patient must swallow the drug or press the button.

Is there any real moral difference between this and the doctor taking the final lethal action? Inevitably, he or she is actively engaged and morally complicit in the destruction of the patient's life. As we will see in a future chapter, this represents a profound reversal in a proud history of over 2,000 years of medical refusal to comply with the deliberate destruction of human lives.

We will now turn to some of the social and economic pressures that lie beneath the current drive for euthanasia and assisted suicide.

4

Underlying forces

Campaigners in favour of assisted suicide sometimes seem to live in an alternative reality. It's a world in which rational people make choices about how they wish to die on the basis of personal preferences, untouched by crude social and economic forces. If elderly and dying people want to choose to end their lives, then we should let them. But in the real world it is very different. As theologian Nigel Biggar has argued, the notion that we are all rational choosers is a flattering lie told to us by people who want to sell us something.

The uncomfortable truth is that much of the time we are influenced and motivated by social and psychological forces that we barely understand. In particular, we must consider the impact of the marked increase in the numbers of elderly and frail people in our midst, and the social, medical and economic pressures which this inevitably creates.

Increasing lifespan

In the UK there are currently about 11 million people over

sixty-five years old. This figure is projected to rise to 15.5 million by 2030, and to around 19 million by 2050. Within this total the number of very old people is growing even faster. There are currently 3 million people aged over eighty years in the UK, and this number is projected to double by 2030, and reach 8 million by 2050. While 1 in 6 of the UK population is currently aged sixty-five and over, by 2050 1 in 4 will be.

And the phenomenon is occurring globally too. People aged sixty years and above account for 11% of the global population. This proportion is expected to double to 22%, or 2 billion people, by 2050. The global number of older people is expected to outstrip the number of youth under sixteen years by 2050. This is not just a phenomenon in rich countries. The fastest growth in the number of elderly people is occurring in developing countries, with profound implications not only for older people themselves, but also for the social and community infrastructure. This is particularly relevant because resources for caring for dying people and providing palliative care are inadequate in most developing countries.

The startling increase in the number of older people is happening at a time when we are seeing a progressive weakening and breakdown of traditional family structures. A UK survey of people over the age of seventy-five found that about 1 in 6 felt socially isolated, and that 42% lived alone, with this figure rising to 72% of those over eighty-five. Many lived long distances from their children and were visited by them just once every two to six months. Some were visited once a year or less. Those in the oldest age cohort were most likely to report the highest rates of loneliness. Over 6 out of 10 of those aged over eighty said they felt lonely. Again, this is not just a rich country phenomenon. A recent study in Bulgaria, Ghana, Nicaragua, Vietnam and the state of Andhra

Pradesh in India reported that between 15% and 30% of older people lived alone or with no adult of working age.

Some social planners see a nightmarish future, where large numbers of isolated and abandoned elderly people are kept alive to suffer a pointless and degrading existence and a lonely death, thanks to improvements in medical care. Wouldn't a liberal euthanasia and assisted-suicide policy provide some kind of solution to this horror?

Health consequences of an ageing population

Improvements in healthcare and medical technology have contributed directly to the increase in lifespan. This is surely a good thing, but it has had unforeseen consequences in increasing the number of elderly people who suffer from chronic health needs. Approximately 20% of those aged seventy years or older, and 50% of people aged eighty-five and over, report difficulties in such basic activities of daily living as bathing, dressing, toileting, continence, feeding, and trans-ferring from chair to bed. As life expectancy increases, so does the likelihood of more years spent in ill health, with women at present suffering on average 11 years, and men 6.7 years, of 'poor health'.

Loneliness also has health consequences, as it is associated with increased mortality, illness, depression and suicide. A 2008 study found that chronic loneliness is a health-risk factor comparable to smoking, obesity and lack of exercise, and con-tributes to a suppressed immune system, high blood pressure and increased levels of the stress hormone cortisol.

Alzheimer's disease and dementia
At the time of writing, about 850,000 people in the UK suffer from dementia, and the Alzheimer's Society predicts that this

figure will increase to over a million by 2021, and 1.7 million by 2051. The proportion of affected individuals in the population is predicted to rise from 16% between seventy-five and eighty-five years to more than 25% over eighty-five years. According to current predictions, someone born now has a 1 in 3 chance of developing some form of dementia before they die. The numbers of people living with dementia worldwide are expected to double every twenty years, and by 2050 it is projected there will be 115 million people with dementia worldwide, 71% of whom will live in developing countries.

In July 2015 newspapers reported the tragic story of a devoted elderly couple, John and Meryl Parry. Meryl had dementia, and John had struggled to care for her at home in a way that respected her dignity. Eventually, Meryl had been admitted to a care home, but John said she was treated 'like a farm animal', and he had taken her back home. Unable to find appropriate emergency care, in desperation he killed her with a plastic bag and pillow over her face.

Finding an appropriate way to care for Alzheimer's sufferers represents a major, and still partly unsolved, challenge for the medical and caring professions. In the Netherlands there is increasing public and medical acceptance that voluntary euthanasia may be appropriate for individuals who are in the early stages of dementia, looking for a way to escape.

Economic consequences of increasing lifespan

Much of the UK government's spending on benefits is focused on elderly people, equivalent to £100 billion in 2010/11 or one seventh of total government spending. The proportion of the UK population who are not employed is expected to rise significantly. In 2008 there were 3.2 people of working age for every person of pensionable age. This ratio is projected to fall to 2.8 by 2033. Continuing to provide state benefits and pensions at today's average would mean an additional spending of £10 billion a year for every additional 1 million people over working age.

Not surprisingly, growing numbers of elderly people are also having an impact on the National Health Service (NHS), where average spending for retired households is nearly double that for non-retired households. The Department of Health estimates that the average cost of providing hospital and community health services for a person aged eighty-five years or more is around three times greater than for a person aged sixty-five to seventy-four years. And the final year of life is often the time when expenditure on healthcare is greatest.

How do these factors influence the assisted-suicide debate?

Most of those who are arguing for a change in the law explicitly distance themselves from any argument based on the potential social and economic benefits which might come from the medically assisted suicide of the elderly and infirm. As we shall see, their arguments are based on an individual's rights to choose the timing and nature of his or her own death, and on compassion towards those who are suffering hopelessly and unbearably.

However, Baroness Mary Warnock is one of the few euthanasia advocates who has been prepared to follow the logic of her position in public. In her book *Easeful Death*, published in 2008, she discusses the benefits of assisted suicide and euthanasia for the elderly and dependent.

> One of the fears most commonly expressed is that, if assisted dying were an option, patients in the last stages of illness

might have pressure put on them to ask for it, when it was not what they really wanted. It is not difficult to imagine feeling that one's children were getting impatient either for their inheritance or simply for relief from the burden of care, and that one had not so much a right to ask for death as a duty to do so, now that it was lawful to provide it. There undoubtedly exist predatory or simply exhausted relatives. But it is insulting to those who ask to be allowed to die to assume that they are incapable of making a genuinely independent choice, free from influence . . .

In any case to ask for death for the sake of one's children or other close relatives can be seen as an admirable thing to do, not in the least indicative of undue pressure, or pressure of any kind. Other kinds of altruism are generally thought worthy of praise. Why should one not admire this final altruistic act? . . . Part of what makes a patient's suffering intolerable may be the sense that he is ruining other people's lives. If he feels this keenly and asks to be allowed to die, he is not a vulnerable victim, but a rational moral agent.

Contemplating the wretched lives of patients with dementia . . . we may feel despair. They are allowed to die, many of them, by a slow and horrible death, far from the 'good death' or the 'death with dignity' that euthanasia would afford them. Many of their relatives, if there are any, must long for them to die . . . What is to be done? This is a question to which, as far as we can see, society can at present supply no answer. But it must be faced as we become an increasingly aged population.

In a widely quoted interview in 2008 Mary Warnock stated,

If you're demented, you're wasting people's lives – your family's lives – and you're wasting the resources of the

National Health Service. I'm absolutely, fully, in agreement with the argument that if pain is insufferable, then someone should be given help to die, but I feel there's a wider argument that if somebody absolutely, desperately, wants to die because they're a burden to their family, or the state, then I think they too should be allowed to die.

Her remarks created a furore, and were strongly opposed by the majority of those who care for Alzheimer's sufferers, but in reality they reflect the unspoken thoughts of many. Faced with the demographic time bomb of an ageing population with its profound social, economic and health risks to the future survival of civilization, maybe legally controlled and medically supervised suicide can provide a solution. Perhaps choosing to kill yourself in old age will come to be seen as the responsible, compassionate and altruistic option.

Euthanasia as an altruistic option

Euthanasia can provide organs for transplantation

The possibility of making a link between euthanasia and the shortage of organs for transplant seemed entirely theoretical until recently. But several cases of organ donation coupled with euthanasia have now been reported from Belgium. In 2005 and 2007 four patients expressed their will for organ donation after their request for euthanasia was granted. They were aged forty-three to fifty years and suffered from a debilitating neurologic disease. According to the published report, 'The euthanasia procedures were carried out on the date requested by the patient, by three physicians independent from procurement or transplant teams, in the operating room. After clinical diagnosis of cardiac death, organ procurement was performed . . .'

In 2012 it was stated that nine cases of organ donation following euthanasia had occurred. A total of 1,100 cases of euthanasia occurred in Belgium in 2011, and it was reported that since the majority of cases were in terminally ill people with cancer, only a small proportion were suitable to be donors. Most people, including most doctors, have an intuitive reaction against the association of euthanasia with organ transplantation, but on strictly utilitarian grounds the argument is clearly persuasive.

Too many people already

Even world overpopulation can be seen as a factor in the trend towards the increasing acceptability of euthanasia and assisted suicide. The current population of the world is over 7 billion, and it is continuing to rise at nearly 2% per annum. Several recent environmental studies have argued that the entire resources of the planet are only sufficient to sustain a significantly smaller population at a European standard of living. This is described as the 'carrying capacity' of the planet – the maximum population size of the species that the environment can sustain indefinitely. If global living standards are to be maintained, and catastrophic climate change is to be avoided, then future generations will have to face the challenge of ensuring a drastic reduction in world population to sustainable levels while avoiding destabilizing violence and social breakdown.

Perhaps the promotion of old-age suicide, maybe with a range of incentives to encourage wide-scale adoption, will provide a solution?

These sinister and dystopic fantasies may seem far-fetched. Those who wish to promote the legalization of medically assisted suicide strongly disassociate themselves from such goals, preferring to concentrate on individual choice and liberties. But it is surely naive to imagine that the enormous challenges raised by a growing and ageing population can be entirely separated from the legalization of medically assisted suicide.

So what are the main arguments that are used to support the legalization of assisted suicide, and why have some prominent Christian clerics come out in support of them? In the next two chapters we now turn to the central issues.

5

The argument from compassion

The fashion designer Jasper Conran, quoted on the Dignity in Dying website, said,

> It seems extraordinary to me that as a nation we operate on a moral double standard. If our pets are hopelessly ill, we have them put down to save them from pain and call that humane. If, however, our nearest and dearest are terminally ill and writhing in an agony that drugs cannot help any more, we allow the law to insist that we do nothing.

Here are the words of Lord Joel Joffe (mentioned earlier), the distinguished lawyer who introduced an Assisted Dying Bill to the House of Lords in 2006: 'I care about suffering and want the law changed so that those who presently suffer terrible deaths will in future have the option to end their suffering through ending their lives at a time and in the manner of their choice.'

In this chapter we focus on what is historically the oldest argument for euthanasia, the argument from compassion. In the next one we focus on the argument from autonomy. As we shall see, these two arguments are persuasive and effective for campaigners because they are based on genuine concerns for the well-being of dying people, concerns that most people share, including Christian believers.

Frankly, the argument from compassion seems simple and compelling. Common humanity demands that we try to reduce the suffering of others, and therefore as a humane society we must provide legal means for individuals to end their suffering by ending their lives.

Christian voices for assisting suicide from compassion

For the Reverend Professor Paul Badham, compassion for those who suffer at the end of life is a central argument in favour of voluntary euthanasia. He quotes from the famous hymn to love in 1 Corinthians 13: 'If I have a faith that can move mountains, but do not have love, I am nothing. If I give all I possess to the poor and give over my body to hardship that I may boast, but do not have love, I gain nothing' (verses 2–3, NIV).

Paul Badham argues, 'It is hard to see how anyone who takes St Paul's praise of loving compassion seriously could fail to respond to the desperate cries for help of terminally ill patients who wish to die.' He emphasizes the importance of Christ's teaching about the Golden Rule, and refers to anecdotal evidence that some doctors make private arrangements to ensure that in the event of terminal illness, they receive covert assistance from colleagues to hasten their own deaths. 'If they were to extend assistance to die to their patients, they would literally be fulfilling Jesus' golden rule of treating others as they wish to be treated themselves.'

As mentioned in the Introduction, Lord Carey, the distinguished past Archbishop of the Church of England, has added his voice in favour of a change in the law. Speaking in the House of Lords' debate in 2014, he said that he had dropped his previous opposition to assisted suicide:

> When suffering is so great that some patients, already knowing that they are at the end of life, make repeated pleas to die, it seems a denial of that loving compassion which is the hallmark of Christianity to refuse to allow them to fulfil their own clearly stated request – after, of course, a proper process of safeguards has been observed. If we truly love our neighbours as ourselves, how can we deny them the death that we would wish for ourselves in such a condition? That is what I would want . . .

So, what's wrong with the argument from compassion?

The argument from compassion sounds compelling and, according to some, entirely consistent with Christian thinking. But it is important to recognize the highly questionable assumptions which lie behind it.

The emotional power of the argument is that, of course, we do have a duty to respond to those who are suffering. Both Christian teaching and common humanity demand that we respond with compassion to 'the desperate cries for help of terminally ill patients'. But is killing the best practical and compassionate response that is available? Can't practical compassion drive us instead to the provision of expert pain relief, psychological support and human companionship through the terminal phases of illness? As we shall see later, one of the wonderful discoveries of modern palliative care was that with skill and dedication, it is possible not only to control physical pain, but also to address the psychological pain, relational pain and spiritual pain so often experienced by dying people.

The pro-euthanasia activists use highly emotive, and frankly manipulative, language which implies that every moment thousands of people are dying in terrible agony – 'suffering terrible deaths, writhing in agony' – but these descriptions do not reflect the experience of experts in palliative medicine. Sadly, at the moment, in the UK and elsewhere across the world, the provision of high-quality palliative care is patchy and inadequate. Because of this, even in modern hospitals and healthcare facilities, it is true that some people do die in severe pain. At the time of writing in 2015 an independent report from the UK Royal College of Physicians found that thousands of patients were 'dying badly' in NHS hospitals every year. Some NHS hospitals were failing to adhere to agreed guidelines on palliative care. But surely, this is a compelling argument for improving palliative care services, not for introducing legalized killing.

Is there a difference between 'unbearable' and 'bearable' suffering?

The argument from compassion provides the bedrock for euthanasia legislation in the Netherlands and Belgium. As we saw, it is the moral and compassionate response of the treating doctor which is the critical factor in these countries. He or she has an absolute medical duty to bring to an end suffering which is 'unbearable and hopeless' by ensuring the death of the patient.

As we have also seen, it is not unusual in the Netherlands for the patient's request for euthanasia to be turned down by his or her doctor because the degree of suffering is regarded as insufficient. So there is clearly an implicit threshold of personal suffering which the doctor must consider prior to agreeing to provide euthanasia. It seems that this represents the threshold between 'unbearable' suffering, which deserves euthanasia, and 'bearable' suffering, which does not.

The implication is that even if a patient pleads to be killed, medical destruction of that life is not morally justified unless this threshold of suffering is reached. But how is the value of an individual life to be weighed against a subjective assessment of suffering by a physician? It is interesting that whereas in earlier versions of proposed assisted suicide legislation in the UK, 'unbearable suffering' was regarded as a prerequisite before medical suicide could be procured, this requirement was removed completely in the recommendations made by the Falconer Commission:

> The Commission does not consider that any criterion based on 'unbearable' or 'unrelievable' suffering should be included in potential assisted-dying legislation, as we are concerned that a criterion based on suffering would be too unclear and subjective for doctors to assess; we believe it is only for the individual concerned to judge the extent of the suffering caused by their illness.

So, to put it rather bluntly, medical killing is only justified in the Netherlands if the doctor determines there is 'unbearable suffering', but there is no requirement to be terminally ill. In the UK it is proposed that medically assisted suicide would be justified if there is terminal illness, and there is no legal requirement to prove to an outsider that you are suffering. The incompatibility of the different legal frameworks points out the arbitrariness of the legal grounds.

The assessment of 'unbearable and hopeless suffering' becomes even more problematic in the case of individuals with psychiatric disorders. As we saw in the comments made by the Dutch psychiatrist in chapter 2, those who regard their lives as unbearable due to anorexia nervosa or untreatable psychotic delusions may legally receive euthanasia in the Netherlands, although this would not be acceptable as grounds for assisted suicide in the UK (unless, unusually, their life expectancy was deemed to be less than six months).

A highly subjective judgment on behalf of the treating clinician and second adviser seems unavoidable in these cases. And if the two doctors have concluded that the suffering is indeed 'unbearable and hopeless', how might that judgment be challenged? Indeed, it seems that the only successful legal challenges to euthanasia acts in the Netherlands have been on the basis of failure to carry out the correct administrative procedure, rather than on the basis of the assessment of suffering.

And how can one assess the tragic case of Nathan, born Nancy, Verhelst, who was killed by lethal injection in Belgium in 2013 after requesting euthanasia on the grounds of 'unbearable psychological suffering'? After a life of being rejected by his parents as a daughter, Mr Verhelst had hormone therapy, followed by mastectomy and unsuccessful surgery to construct a penis in 2012. Verhelst stated that surgery to turn him into a man had resulted in 'a monster'.

The shaky logic of euthanasia legislation

At present euthanasia legislation in the Netherlands and Belgium restricts medical killing to those who enjoy a certain degree of intellectual function. But if a physician has a moral duty out of compassion to end the unbearable suffering of a legally competent adult, it is hard to see why there is not an equivalent duty to end the suffering of a patient who lacks intellectual and legal capacity, such as a person with brain injury or severe psychotic delusions, or a suffering child or baby. If there is a moral duty from compassion to end unbearable suffering, then why should this be restricted only to competent adults?

In the UK there is also a startling illogicality in restricting assisted suicide to those who have a terminal illness and are likely to die from natural causes within six months. At least in these cases those who are suffering know that death is imminent; their suffering is going to come to an end. Surely we should have greater compassion towards those who are suffering unbearably but who have no prospect of dying from natural causes? In these cases the suffering is likely to go on year after year. Don't these tragic people demand our compassion too? On what logical grounds can we exclude such people from assisted suicide while offering it to those who are about to die?

Arguments for compassionate killing have also been used in two other circumstances. First, there are those who are not physically suffering, but who passionately wish to die because they feel their lives are 'not worth living'. Secondly, there are those who are not suffering in any recognizable way, but an external observer concludes that their lives are purposeless and futile – those in coma from severe brain injury, individuals with advanced dementia, the severely malformed newborn infant. Should not compassion lead us to end these futile lives? This, of course, was the argument used in Nazi Germany that led to the euthanasia programme.

'Compassion' has been used to justify horrific crimes

Dr Karl Brandt, Hitler's personal physician who led the euthanasia programme, explained his motivation at the Nuremberg War Trials:

The underlying motive was the desire to help individuals who could not help themselves and were thus prolonging their lives in torment. To quote Hippocrates today is to proclaim that invalids and persons in great pain should never be given poison. But any modern doctor who makes so rhetorical a declaration without qualification is a liar or hypocrite . . . I never intended anything more or believed I was doing anything but abbreviating the tortured existence of such unhappy creatures.

It is all too apparent that 'compassion' is a slippery concept, and that it has been used within living memory to justify the most horrific crimes. Still, the argument from compassion seems to have considerable persuasive power for modern people. And yet it is ironic that we live in an era of unparalleled advances in techniques for treating and controlling pain and other distressing symptoms. Indeed, the treatment available for dying people has advanced remarkably in the last thirty to forty years.

Are we more compassionate than we used to be?

The argument from compassion has special resonance for Christians and others of good will, because it seems to chime with a deep instinct about responding to those in desperate need. For 2,000 years Christian believers and communities have been responding with compassion to those suffering severe and uncontrollable pain at the end of life. And yet Christian compassion did not drive those believers to help patients to kill themselves. So why is it now, at this particular time when pain relief and palliative care have become so effective, that Archbishop Carey feels compelled to change his mind? Are we more compassionate than our Christian sisters and brothers have been over the last 2,000 years? Why does the argument from compassion seem so conclusive at this point in history?

Can suffering have any positive value?

It seems that one of the novel features of our modern technological and liberal society is that we have lost the belief that suffering can have any positive value at all. Pain, whether physical, mental, relational or spiritual, is seen as useless, futile, destructive, incomprehensible, terrifying. It is not surprising that utilitarianism, perhaps the most influential form of moral thinking underpinning modern secularism, defines pain as the greatest moral evil in the universe. Conversely, anything that reduces and minimizes the sum total of human suffering represents the greatest possible good.

This utilitarian thinking has penetrated deeply into modern culture. The ultimate purpose of existence is to maximize personal happiness, and if we can't be happy, then at least we can try to anaesthetize the pain. So all forms of anaesthesia become potent, desirable and morally acceptable. Alcohol, recreational drugs, entertainment, retail therapy – they all help to numb the pain. And when we face our own mortality, we respond in the same way. When asked how we would wish to die, the commonest answer is: 'I want to die in my sleep, with no awareness, no discomfort, no anticipation, no warning.' But if in reality we don't die in this desirable way, then, 'Just put me out of it, doc. Put me to sleep. I don't want to come round. I don't want to know what's happening.'

So suicide and euthanasia become highly desirable because they seem to guarantee freedom from pain. They are the ultimate form of anaesthesia, and hence, in a strange way, the ultimate moral good.

Your 'compassion' may threaten my life

'Compassion' is an ambiguous concept, and one that can easily become confused and incoherent. If I am in the depths of suffering and despair, then it is surely right that I should be treated with compassion by others. My safety and security as a vulnerable and dependent human being rest on your compassion. But if your 'compassion' might motivate you to end my life, then something seems to have changed. We saw this in the tragic story of the devoted elderly couple John and Meryl Parry in a previous chapter. John was genuinely motivated by compassion. He was appalled at the short-comings of the care that Meryl was receiving, being treated like a 'farm animal'. But his compassion meant that her life was at threat, and it ended in her killing. Just when I am most vulnerable and dependent, am I at risk from the 'compassion' of others?

The core meaning of compassion: 'It's good that you are alive'

So what is the core meaning of compassion? In Christian understanding it is closely linked to love for the other – practical concern for the very best for the other person. And at its most fundamental, Christian love says to that person, 'It's good that you exist; it's good that you are in the world', to use the words of the philosopher Josef Pieper. The problem with euthanasia and assisted suicide is that in effect they say precisely the opposite: 'It's bad that you exist. It would be much better if you were not in the world.'

Does this mean that when faced with unbearable and hopeless suffering in another, we must just harden our heart? Is our natural instinct towards compassionate action misguided and dangerous? No, on the contrary, we must always act with genuine compassion towards the suffering one. But true compassion, when directed by wisdom and judgment, points away from killing and in another direction. Cicely Saunders and the other pioneers of palliative care were extremely concerned to find ways of controlling both physical and other forms of pain, and they discovered that with skilled modern medical care, *it is not necessary to kill the patient in order to kill the pain.* Compassion for the agonies of suffering people with terminal illness was the primary driving force behind the development of modern palliative care, but it led not to medical killing, but to caring – skilled, costly and life-affirming.

It is not necessary to kill the patient in order to kill the pain.

In a later chapter we will see more about how modern palliative care provides compassionate and practical ways of caring for dying people. But now we will turn to the other main argument for a change in the law, the powerful argument that resonates most deeply with people in the twenty-first century.

6

The argument from autonomy

I believe passionately that any individual should have the right to choose, as far as it is possible, the time and the conditions of their death. I think it's time we learned to be as good at dying as we are at living.

(Terry Pratchett)

On the surface it all seems so very simple. Human beings have the right to choose – end of story. If we can control every other aspect of our lives – where we live, how we spend our money, who we decide to marry – then surely we have the right to end our own lives whenever and however we choose. 'Whose life is it anyway?'

The philosophers call this the principle of 'autonomy', a word derived from the Greek *auto-nomos*, meaning self-rule, or more crudely, 'I make my own laws.' Some experts in medical ethics have argued that the principle of autonomy has become the single most important principle in all medical decision-making. Every and any other consideration must take second place.

Autonomy is the principle behind patient choice, the touch-stone of modern healthcare. It is enshrined in the Patient Charter, the NHS Constitution, the Mental Capacity Act and in General Medical Council guidelines for doctors. It is the patient who should be at the centre, choosing and controlling what treatment should be given. And considering that we have the right to make choices about every other aspect of our medical treatment, why do we not have the right of self-rule when it comes to when and how we die?

Here's philosopher A. C. Grayling on the subject:

I believe that decisions about the timing and manner of death belong to the individual as a human right. I believe it is wrong to withhold medical methods of terminating life painlessly and swiftly when an individual has a rational and clear-minded sustained wish to end his or her life.

Philosopher John Harris has a slightly different take, arguing that shaping our own lives for ourselves is what gives value to our own existence: 'Autonomy, as the ability and the freedom to make the choices that shape our lives, is quite crucial in giving to each life its own special and peculiar value.'

If I am genuinely the master of my fate, then surely that must mean I have the right to choose to end my life.

Others have argued that each life should be like a beautiful novel. Any individual's way of death should fit with how that person has lived the rest of their life. Otherwise, a bad death might mar the whole story of a life, just as a bad ending can ruin a beautiful novel. If I have lived my life by choosing, taking responsibility for my own existence, telling my own story, then I must be free to end my life in my own way, in a way that fits.

I am the captain of my soul

This attitude of self-mastery is portrayed most vividly in the Victorian poem 'Invictus', which has been adopted by several prominent politicians, including Nelson Mandela:

> Out of the night that covers me,
> Black as the Pit from pole to pole,
> I thank whatever gods may be
> For my unconquerable soul.
>
> In the fell clutch of circumstance
> I have not winced nor cried aloud.
> Under the bludgeonings of chance
> My head is bloody, but unbowed.
>
> Beyond this place of wrath and tears
> Looms but the Horror of the shade,
> And yet the menace of the years
> Finds, and shall find, me unafraid.
>
> It matters not how strait the gate,
> How charged with punishments the scroll.
> I am the master of my fate:
> I am the captain of my soul.
> (William Ernest Henley, 1849–1902)

These high-flown sentiments resonate with many in our society. If I am genuinely the master of my fate, then surely that must mean I have the right to choose to end my life.

The individual is king

This modern fixation can be traced back to the Enlightenment philosopher John Stuart Mill. In his 1865 book *On Liberty* he wrote, 'The only purpose for which power can be rightfully exercised over any member of a civilized community against his will, is to prevent harm to others . . . Over himself, over his body and mind, the individual is sovereign.'

The wording is significant. There are other sovereigns in the public or political realm, but in private life and morality the individual is sovereign. In eighteenth-century Europe the political concept of the sovereign nation state was being developed. In Mill's thought each individual becomes their own nation state with their own sovereign, although Mill did not approve of suicide. From the perspective of traditional Western thought, freedom was an essential precondition for people to choose what is good. But in modern liberal societies it is choice which becomes a good in itself – in fact, for many it is the supreme good.

Philosopher Ronald Dworkin argues that individual control over the manner and timing of our death is of central importance to everyone:

> Death has dominion because it is not only the start of
> nothing but the end of everything, and how we think
> and talk about dying – the emphasis we put on dying
> with 'dignity' – shows how important it is that life ends
> appropriately, that death keeps faith with the way we
> want to have lived.

He argues that we worry about dying in indignity, 'as we might worry about the effect of a play's last scene, or a poem's last stanza, on the entire creative work'.

People's views about how to live colour their convictions about when to die . . . There is no doubt that most people treat the manner of their deaths as of special, symbolic importance: they want their deaths, if possible, to express and . . . confirm the values they believe most important to their lives . . . None of us wants to end our life out of character.

Christian voices arguing for choice and control over death

Just like the argument from compassion, the argument from autonomy seems attractive to many Christian believers because it seems to chime with deep and genuine principles of the faith – in this case a deep concern for human freedom.

Desmond Tutu, the distinguished South African archbishop and campaigner against apartheid whom we met earlier, stated in 2014 that laws that prevent people from being helped to end their lives were an affront to those affected and their families. He condemned as 'disgraceful' the treatment of his old friend Nelson Mandela, who was kept alive through numerous painful hospitalizations and forced to endure a photo stunt with politicians shortly before his death at ninety-five.

Tutu called for a 'mind shift' in the right-to-die debate: 'I have been fortunate to spend my life working for dignity for the living. Now I wish to apply my mind to the issue of dignity for the dying. I revere the sanctity of life – but not at any cost.'

So a genuine concern for the dignity of dying people leads Desmond Tutu to conclude that they must have a legal right to end their own lives. But is self-destruction a truly dignified way to die?

Respect for autonomy in English law

Respect for individual autonomy is certainly highly regarded in modern medical and legal practice. In a landmark case, that of Miss B, the English High Court accepted that an individual patient could legally insist that life-sustaining treatment should be withdrawn. Due to bleeding into the spinal cord, Miss B, a forty-one-year-old social worker, developed progressive paralysis from the neck down. Because of increasing breathing difficulties, she was transferred to an intensive care unit, and life-support treatment with artificial ventilation was commenced. Treatment attempts failed, and Miss B remained dependent on a mechanical ventilator. Miss B repeatedly asked the doctors caring for her to switch off the life-support machinery so that she could die.

The case was referred to the High Court, and in a remarkable precedent the Court held part of its proceedings within the intensive care unit so that the patient could give evidence in person. Dame Elizabeth Butler-Sloss, the presiding judge, expressed her admiration for Miss B's courage, strength of will and determination. 'She is a splendid person, and it is tragic that someone of her ability has been struck down so cruelly. I hope she will forgive me for saying, diffidently, that if she did reconsider her decision, she would have a lot to offer the community at large.'

Dame Elizabeth concluded that Miss B did indeed have the mental capacity to refuse treatment, and that the hospital, by continuing to treat her with ventilation against her wishes, had acted unlawfully. 'One must allow for those as severely disabled as Miss B, for some of whom life in that condition may be worse than death.' Interestingly, the doctors at the original hospital were not compelled by force of law to withdraw the treatment they had started, against their own conscience. Instead, Miss B was moved to another hospital, where shortly afterwards intensive treatment was withdrawn at her request and she died.

This judgment has been highly influential, confirming the right of competent patients to refuse life-sustaining treatment. But should the same respect for autonomy lead to a conclusion that there should be a legal right for patients to kill themselves?

Autonomy is not as simple as it sounds

As we saw at the beginning of the chapter, Terry Pratchett argued that everybody had the right to control the time and manner of their death. Yet this argument is not as simple as it sounds. Was Terry Pratchett really arguing that we should assist people to destroy their own lives, under any circumstances and for any reason whatsoever? What kind of society would it be that assisted people to kill themselves whenever they wished? A society that provided lethal medications for depressed individuals with suicidal thoughts, that provided humane alternative methods of self-destruction for people threatening to throw themselves off a cliff or in front of a train, that made suicide an easy process for lonely, elderly, disabled or despairing people. Is this the kind of society that is being proposed, and is this a society that we would honestly wish to belong to?

In reality, virtually all those arguing in favour of assisting people to kill themselves add a number of additional criteria that must be met, additional barriers that must be circumvented, before we will provide a legal method to assist people to destroy themselves. Here are some of the additional criteria that have been proposed:

Additional barriers proposed

a. The choice to kill oneself should be an enduring and persisting one

This barrier recognizes that suicidal thoughts may be transitory and impulsive. The Falconer Commission recommended that

> a person would only initiate the process of requesting an assisted death after considerable discussion with their doctor . . . it is important that some time should be built into the process to ensure that the patient's decision cannot be made hastily, and that it is a settled decision to die, as opposed to a fluctuating wish . . . The proposed safeguard is that a minimum time period of two weeks must elapse between the request being made by the subject, and the assisted death occurring.

This may seem like common sense, but it is an obvious restriction on the right of self-governance. If I am overwhelmed by grief and despair, and wish to kill myself immediately here and now, on what logical grounds am I denied that right? Why must I be forced to endure a further two weeks of mental anguish? The demand for a 'settled', 'enduring' or 'persistent' decision is a recognition that free choice alone is not enough.

b. The choice to kill oneself must not be the consequence of mental illness

It is very well known that 'suicidal ideation', recurring thoughts about killing oneself, is an extremely common symptom of depressive mental illness. The members of the Falconer Commission concluded,

Although the distinction between 'appropriate sadness' and depression in the context of terminal illness is complex, the Commission does not consider that a person with depression, whose judgement might be significantly impaired as a result of this depression, should be permitted to take such a momentous decision as ending their own life . . .

It seems very likely that the great majority of people who choose to kill themselves out of despair, because they feel that their lives are worthless, have at least some elements of what most of us would recognize as depression, 'low self-worth' or persistently low mood. But even if my choice to kill myself is a reflection of depression, it is still my choice. As we have seen, in the Netherlands assisted suicide has been provided on occasion for those with severe and long-lasting depression. A 2015 paper in the *Journal of Medical Ethics*, written by two Dutch philosophers, argued strongly for the right of patients with treatment-resistant depression to be helped to kill themselves. To exclude such patients from assisted suicide was unfair discrimination.

And then there is the complex and painful issue of dementia. Suppose that I am in the early stages of dementia. I still have some degree of rational ability, but I realize that in front of me lies the inevitable prospect of progressive mental deterioration. I will never again live an independent life; there will be greater and greater demands on my loved ones and carers. If at this point I choose to make a living will, an advance directive that I wish to be killed if I become completely mentally incapacitated in the future, then surely this is a free autonomous decision which should be supported and facilitated?

Yet many supporters of autonomous choice have drawn back here. The Falconer Commission concluded,

We are sympathetic as a Commission to those people who are in the early stages of dementia, who might appreciate the security of knowing they could specify in a legal document the circumstances in which they would like to be able to end their life, once they had lost capacity. However, we consider that the requirement of mental capacity is an essential safeguard for assisted dying legislation; therefore the Commission does not propose any legislation that might allow non-competent people to receive assistance in ending their lives.

c. The choice to kill oneself must not be the consequence of coercion or manipulation

The rhetoric of self-determination sounds compelling from the philosopher's chair or the politician's rousing speech – 'I am the master of my fate: I am the captain of my soul', as the poem asserted. But in the complexities of human relationships and the play of tragic circumstances, it is not so simple. Our choices, wishes and desires are all influenced by the web of relationships in which we find ourselves. Is it not possible that my choice to be killed is being influenced by the wishes of others?

The Falconer Commission recognized that there was a significant danger in this area:

> The Commission accepts that there is a real risk that some individuals might come under pressure to request an assisted death if this option should become available, including direct pressures from family members or medical professionals, indirect pressures caused by societal discrimination or lack of availability of resources for care and support, and self-imposed pressures that could result from the individuals having low self-worth or feeling themselves to be a burden on others.

The Commission does not accept that any of these forms of pressure could be a legitimate motivation for a terminally ill individual to seek an assisted death. Therefore, it is essential that any future system should contain safeguards designed to ensure, as much as possible, that any decision to seek an assisted suicide is a genuinely voluntary and autonomous choice, not influenced by another person's wishes, or by constrained social circumstances, such as lack of access to adequate end-of-life care and support.

But although this is clearly well-meaning, it is also, frankly, absurd. How can we ever be confident that a choice to kill oneself is not influenced by other people's wishes or by limitations in the social support available? In the state of Oregon, in published reports, between 40% and 60% of those requesting doctor-assisted suicide cited 'Burden on family, friends/caregivers' as a reason. (As we saw earlier, Mary Warnock argued that this was an entirely appropriate reason for wishing to kill oneself.)

It is common to find elderly people who are concerned that they are becoming an unwanted burden on their relatives and carers. Desiring to act responsibly and altruistically, they may come to perceive that it would be better for everybody if their life were to end. There is a deep and tragic irony that it is precisely those elderly people who are most sensitive to the needs and concerns of others who may be most at risk of being emotionally manipulated into taking their own lives.

Elderly people who are most sensitive to the concerns of others are at most risk of being manipulated into taking their own lives.

And can we, or others, always detect the covert influences and emotional factors which lie behind our choices? In the words of Nigel Biggar previously referred to, 'The notion that we are all rational choosers is a flattering lie told us by people who want to sell us something.' If Freud has taught the heirs of modernity anything, it is the uncomfortable truth that much of the time we are influenced and motivated by social and psychological forces that we barely understand.

d. The choice to kill oneself must be 'rational' or 'well-founded'

Even if our choice is persistent, not arising from mental illness and genuinely free, another barrier has been constructed which we must circumvent if we are to receive assistance. Our decision to die must be 'rational'. But what exactly is a rational reason to destroy your own life?

Since many philosophers conceive of death as the cessation of all autonomous action, there is a certain irony (if not logical incoherence) in the idea that the triumph of autonomy should lead to the premature destruction of that self-same autonomy. Surely, those who wish to promote autonomy as the supreme good should oppose the squandering of this ultimate value in self-destruction.

As we saw in chapter 3, both the USA and the UK have turned against mercy killing by doctors in favour of assisted suicide. This Anglo-Saxon model has assumed that the only acceptable rational reason to wish to die is terminal illness, in other words, the apparent certainty that natural death is only a matter of weeks or at most months away. The Falconer Commission stated that the only people who would be eligible would be those who had an advanced, progressive, incurable condition that was likely to lead to the patient's death within the next twelve months. This was subsequently changed in the Assisted Dying Bill of 2014 to a reasonable expectation of death from a terminal illness within six months, although the reason behind the halving of life expectancy required for legal suicide is opaque, and it seems to be guided more by political pragmatism than by moral principle. The change from twelve to six months illustrates the arbitrariness of this vital definition for the proposed law.

Every experienced doctor knows that predicting life expectancy is fraught with uncertainty, and failed predictions are frequent and inevitable. But leaving this practical problem aside, it seems strange that the only rationally acceptable reason for killing oneself is terminal illness.

Problems with defining rational reasons for suicide

If we once accept that there may be rational reasons to wish to kill yourself, then many might argue that severe, continuous and intractable physical suffering provided a more understandable reason than the knowledge that you were going to die anyway within six months. Just think of those tragic stories from the first chapter: locked-in sufferer Tony Nicklinson, or Daniel James, paralysed from the chest downwards. Surely their suffering would provide equally rational reasons for suicide.

As we saw in chapter 3, the Falconer Commission explicitly rejected disability as grounds for assisted suicide. Since this is a critical issue, it is worth re-examining the wording of their report:

> The intention of the Commission in recommending that any future legislation should permit assisted suicide exclusively for those who are terminally ill and specifically excluding disabled people (unless they are terminally ill) is to establish a clear delineation between the application of assisted suicide to

people who are terminally ill and others with long-term
conditions or impairments . . . The adoption of this distinction
in any future legislation would send a clear message that
disabled people's lives are valued equally . . .

But this seems rather strange. Disabled people's lives are
valued equally (and hence they are protected), but terminally
ill patients' lives are not valued equally, and hence they may
be killed. It's hard to see a logical and rational basis for this
distinction.

It is possible to construct many other apparently rational
grounds for wishing to kill oneself: the desire of an elderly
person to cease to be an expensive burden to his or her
children, the wish of someone facing progressive dementia to
find a way out, or the elderly and lonely person, like Nan
Maitland, who is merely 'tired of life'; all these motivations
seem rational in some sense.

So the restriction of assisted suicide to those who qualify
under an arbitrary definition of terminal illness smacks of
political expediency. In private, many pro-euthanasia campaigners will agree that they regard the proposed legislation
as merely the first step in a future programme of progressive
liberalization of the laws governing the end of life. Once the
principle is accepted that *some* lives can be ended on rational
grounds, then it is hard to see a logical basis on which progressive liberalization can be resisted.

Individualism – I am at the centre of the universe

As we saw earlier, the argument for autonomy rests ultimately
on a profound individualism which stems historically from
the European Enlightenment. In the nineteenth-century
vision of John Stuart Mill each person is like a nation state

with a single sovereign. Human communities represent a kind of United Nations in which we enter into alliances, contracts and disputes between sovereign states. But this is a terribly bleak vision of society, one in which a collection of individuals are making autonomous choices, striving for their own goals. Although Mill emphasized the requirement not to cause harm to others, this moral vision so easily reduces to an infantile 'I do whatever I like, and no-one is going to stop me . . .' Welcome to the ethics of the kindergarten. (In the next chapter I will argue that this view of society is a modern fantasy that fails to recognize the inescapable realities of what it means to be human.)

Fear of dependence

The emphasis on individual choice as the ultimate expression of my identity and self-worth leads on to a deep fear, that of dependence. Once I depend upon another, then the heroic individualism of 'Invictus' comes crashing down. Dependence is threatening and dehumanizing precisely because it threatens my sense of identity, my sense that my life is worth living.

People who have lived their lives as an expression of self-determination and self-reliance are horrified by the prospect that their death might express a completely contrary reality of dependence on others. Instead, they want to be free to die as they wish, even if that form of dying is not what others might wish.

Is sudden death the best way to go?

One way in which many modern people cope with deep-rooted fears about dependence and indignity at the end of life is to hope for a rapid and unexpected death. Yet to many previous generations, sudden death was seen as one of the worst ways to die. To be catapulted into eternity without preparation, without a chance of asking forgiveness for past failings, unable to say goodbye to loved ones, unable to make provision for those who remained, this was viewed with horror by our forebears. Some saw sudden death as evidence of God's judgment on a godless life. But to modern people, sudden death has become the ideal. The catastrophic accident, the sudden cardiac arrest: 'Well, at least he went quickly, never knew what hit him, lucky beggar. I hope I go like that.'

In a later chapter I will argue that a good death is not necessarily a sudden death, and that, paradoxically, many people have discovered that the last days of a life can be the richest, the most intense and the most significant.

But if we do not go quickly, if we have to face a slow, protracted dying, then we want to be killed or to kill ourselves. That way, we do not need to be afraid. We can relax. Provided that euthanasia or assisted suicide is there as an option, we can face our death with equanimity. There will be someone there to help. This is the answer to our deepest fears.

Respecting the rights and needs of others

It is clear that there is a resolute minority in our society who wish to claim their autonomous right to kill themselves at the time and in the manner of their own choosing. But in a humane and just society we must balance their individual rights against the risks of collateral harm to a large number of other individuals.

It is important to remember that only a tiny number of people in the UK travel abroad for assisted suicide compared with the hundreds of thousands who receive medical care at the end of life each year. It is undoubtedly true that there are a large number of older and frail people who want to carry on living despite a terminal diagnosis, but who are vulnerable to wondering whether ending their own life might be a mercy for their relatives and care-givers.

Despite the modern emphasis on individual rights, it is widely recognized that in a civilized and humane society my rights of individual autonomy must frequently be curtailed to respect the needs and vulnerabilities of others. My autonomy as a driver is constantly curtailed by the need to respect traffic laws in order to protect others. My autonomous right to freedom of speech in a public place is curtailed by the legal requirement to avoid hate-speech that will damage others. If I contract a highly lethal infection such as Ebola virus, my right to be free to travel is legally curtailed for the good of others.

So it is surely reasonable that the autonomous desire of a small number of resolute, vocal and determined individuals to have a legal and medically supervised means of killing themselves may have to be curtailed if it exposes large numbers of vulnerable people to the risk of lethal harm. The individual autonomy of a few cannot, and must not, trump all other considerations.

In the next chapter we turn from the individualist thinking of the Enlightenment to that of the historic Christian faith. Christians, too, must be concerned to encourage and enhance genuine freedom. But our understanding of freedom is radically different from that of the Enlightenment. Christian freedom is freedom within the God-given limits of the created order. We cannot free ourselves from the givenness of our human nature. Instead, we find true freedom in becoming the people we were meant to be.

7

Christian responses and perspectives

'I am the master of my fate,' proclaimed William Henley and countless millions of proud individualists after him. But authentic Christian faith starts with a humble and humbling acceptance that there is an objective reality that is outside ourselves, and that is greater than us. I am not the centre of my own universe. I am part of a bigger narrative. The ultimate meaning of our human nature is given to us by our Creator, and the way of wisdom is to live our lives in tune with the way that we and the rest of the universe have been made. As theologian Gilbert Meilaender put it, 'We are most ourselves not when we seek to direct and control our destiny, but when we recognize and admit that our life is grounded in and sustained by God.'

> *I am not the centre of my own universe. I am part of a bigger narrative.*

Freedom to be the person I was made to be

A Christian understanding of freedom is not freedom *from* the created order, but freedom that comes from respecting the nature of our creation. It is only in this way that I am truly free, free to become the person that God created me to be. To use a simplistic analogy, a fish is free to be itself when it is in the ocean. But the fish that chooses to dispense with a watery environment is not so much free as asphyxiating!

As we attempt to develop an authentic Christian response to assisted suicide and other forms of medical killing, we need to start with an understanding of creation, and in particular of the created moral order, the moral principles that God has embedded into the structure of the universe. God did not just create the physical stuff of the universe – atoms and molecules and photons. He also created a hidden moral order, like the grain imprinted in a piece of wood. What it means to be human – and what it means to destroy human life – is not ours to create and invent; *it is given to us*. It is part of the created order, of the way that things are. And true freedom is to live your life along the grain of the deep hidden order of the creation.

To many modern ears, this is outrageous and unacceptable. People demand the right to make themselves whatever they choose. The idea of the created order is seen as a straitjacket, a constricting, limiting and demeaning force. So the modern understanding of freedom is that we should have the right to be freed from the limitations of the created order. We want to break out from those old rules and make up new rules for ourselves. But the truth is that I can only be truly free if I become the person that God created me to be. Christian freedom is freedom to be truly myself.

Made in God's image

'God said, "Let us make mankind in our image . . ."' (Genesis 1:26, NIV). This foundational statement in the first chapter of the Old Testament tells us that human beings are not self-explanatory. Our ultimate identity cannot be derived by careful analysis of our genetic make-up, our anatomical structures, our brain mechanisms or our social history. We are reflections of another reality, and we derive our meaning from outside ourselves, from God, in whose reflection we are made.

Because human beings are made in God's image, we do not need to earn the right to be treated as God-like beings. Our dignity is intrinsic, in the way we have been made, in how God remembers us and calls us. So biblical ethics, the way we are called to treat one another, is derived from biblical anthropology, the way we are made.

The desperate modern attempt to be a totally autonomous individual, constantly creating myself by the decisions and choices I make, is out of touch with reality. It is a modern fantasy. In truth, we are derivative: we are reflections of another reality. And this way of thinking confronts us with the radical nature of our dependence.

I did not choose to be a human being, to be a particular kind of carbon-based life form. I did not choose this form of embodiment, this frailty and these limitations. I did not choose my genetic inheritance, the structures of my body and brain, the nature of my conscious awareness, my sensory experiences and so on. These, whether I like them or not, are part of the given-ness of what it means to be a human being.

And I was not born as an isolated individual. I came into the world locked into a network of relations I did not choose, with a mother and father, grandparents, siblings, aunts and uncles, friends and carers. You and I came into the world utterly dependent on the love and care of people we did not choose. And in Christian thinking this was not some bizarre fluke or accident; it was an essential part of what it means to be human. An integral part of our created humanity is the reality that we are dependent on others; we are designed to depend on one another.

The narrative of a human life

We come into the world as helpless beings, totally dependent on another's love and care. We go through a phase of our lives when other people depend on us. We protect them, care for them, feed them, pay for them. And then most of us will end our physical lives totally dependent on the love and care of others. We will need other people to feed us, protect us and care for us. And this is not a terrible, degrading inhuman reality. It's part of the design. It is a part of the narrative of a human life.

This was brought home to me in a striking way in an incident I have referred to in a previous book. My mother had become totally dependent on twenty-four-hour nursing care as a result of a tragic and rapidly progressive dementing illness. I was visiting her towards the end, and someone put a yoghurt pot and teaspoon into my hand. I tried to feed her. 'Open wide, here it comes . . .' And the thought struck me that this was exactly what she used to do with me, all those years ago. I could remember her words as she fed me. But now the tables were turned. And I remember thinking at the time, 'Perhaps this is the way it was meant to be.' I was learning more of what it meant to be a son, and she was learning more of what it meant to be a mother. Because dependence is part of the story, part of the narrative of the human lives that have been given to us.

Designed to be dependent

In the words of Gilbert Meilaender, 'We are dependent beings, and to think otherwise – to make independence our project, however sincerely – is to live a lie, it is to fly in the face of reality.'

Even in our years of adult 'independence', in reality we remain dependent beings. As I write these words, I am dependent from moment to moment on the activities and contributions of countless other human beings – on people who generate electricity to power my laptop, on those who grow, prepare, transport and sell food for me to eat, on people who purify water and remove waste, on police and security personnel who protect me ceaselessly from harm, and so on.

In biblical thinking our radical dependence extends to the Creator God who knows and sustains every atom of our being. In the depth of his suffering and loss, the biblical character Job reflects on this theme:

> Your hands fashioned me and made me,
>   and now you have destroyed me altogether.
> Remember that you have made me like clay;
>   and will you return me to the dust?
> Did you not pour me out like milk
>   and curdle me like cheese?
> You clothed me with skin and flesh,
>   and knit me together with bones and sinews.
> You have granted me life and steadfast love,
>   and your care has preserved my spirit.
> (Job 10:8–12)

Being a burden to others

As we have seen, one of the greatest fears expressed by elderly or disabled people is that they will be a burden to others. And in Oregon and elsewhere this is a frequent reason that elderly people give for requesting assisted suicide. But in God's creation order we are meant to be a burden to one another! This is part of what it means to belong to a family, or to a community. Paul commanded the Galatians, as members of the Christian family, to 'carry each other's burdens, and in this way you will fulfil the law of Christ' (Galatians 6:2, NIV). To be called into a family is to be called to share the burdens of the life which God has given us, the burdens which come from our creation out of dust. The life of a family, including the Christian church family, should be one of 'mutual burdensomeness'.

> *But in God's creation order we are meant to be a burden to one another!*

Of course, this is profoundly countercultural in a society that, at least in theory, prizes heroic individualism and self-governance. Yet here is an opportunity for the Christian community to model a different way of being fully human.

Biblical thought always draws a line between removing suffering and removing the sufferer. Yes, we have an absolute duty to care for our suffering neighbour. Yes, we should be motivated by Christian compassion, following the example of Jesus Christ. But no, we are not at liberty to destroy innocent human life, however noble the motive may be. The sixth commandment, 'You shall not murder' (Exodus 20:13), provides an absolute moral imperative, which we cannot evade.

Here are the solemn words of the *lex talionis* in the book of Genesis, said to be one of the earliest known legal statutes in the entire world literature:

Whoever sheds the blood of man,
   by man shall his blood be shed,
for God made man in his own image.
(Genesis 9:6)

As many commentators have pointed out, this ancient text combines two biblical themes. First, there is the ancient blood taboo, a recognition of the special status of blood because it represents a spilled life, and secondly, there is the recognition of the special status of murder, the intentional destruction of innocent human life which is linked to the indwelling image of God. To destroy human life is uniquely scandalous because it is a desecration of God's image, God's masterpiece.

The Christian view of a human life as a gift received from God is often caricatured by opponents. God is the slave-owner, and humans are his slaves, and therefore God 'owns' each life. We are not free to dispose of our own life as we wish, because God 'owns' it. But this is a distortion of the biblical view. We are not merely slaves. Human beings are special because of how they are made – because they are a mysterious expression of God's being.

How should Christians regard suicide?

Orthodox Christian thought has always been opposed not only to homicide, the taking of another human life, but also to suicide. The deliberate destruction of one's own life is also a desecration of God's image. In many ancient cultures suicide has been glorified as a noble way to die, the death of a nobleman, the death of a hero. In ancient Greece the Stoics supported suicide as justifiable and virtuous under circumstances when happiness was not possible.

Cicero, the prominent Stoic philosopher, wrote, 'When a man's circumstances contain a preponderance of things in accordance with nature, it is appropriate for him to remain alive; when he possesses or sees in prospect a majority of the contrary things, it is appropriate for him to depart from life.' But in all cultures influenced by the Judeo-Christian revelation, suicide has been opposed. It is never glorified in the Bible, but instead is seen as an act of hopelessness and despair, for example, in the tragic ends of King Saul, the first king of Israel, and Judas Iscariot. Despite this, it is clear that suicidal thoughts are not uncommon in God's people. Elijah wanted to die, but was sent on a sabbatical instead. Jeremiah wishes he had died in his mother's womb, but discovers that God has plans for welfare and not for evil, to give 'a future and a hope' (see Jeremiah 29:11). Job, too, wishes he had never been born, but learns that God is infinitely greater than his own perceptions.

So suicidal thoughts are not unusual in God's people, but suicide itself is not honoured and glorified because human life is worth more than that. Both intentional killing and suicide are ultimately contrary to the Christian understanding of reality. Even when tempted to kill out of compassion, we come up against the limits of our creatureliness.

Human intuitions about the destruction of human life

But it is not only those with an explicit Christian faith who sense a profound resistance to the taking of human life. The unease and distress expressed by many doctors and healthcare workers who have participated in euthanasia or assisted suicide are themselves evidence of deep intuitions about the special nature of human life – intuitions which stem from our creation in God's image.

Studies of doctors who have performed euthanasia and assisted suicide in the Netherlands and USA have shown high levels of temporary emotional discomfort, distress and a sense of burdensomeness. In the words of one Dutch doctor, 'To kill someone is something far reaching and that is something that nags at your conscience . . . I wonder what it would be like not to have these cases in my practice. Perhaps I would be a much more cheerful person.'

Another Dutch family doctor described how he always tried to resist a request for euthanasia from one of his patients. Whenever the pressure became unbearable, he would arrange for euthanasia to be performed on a Friday afternoon. Afterwards his habit was to go for long walks in the country-side; he would read poetry, listen to Bach, and try generally to prepare himself emotionally for starting work again on the following Monday morning.

'It is not a normal medical treatment. You are never used to it.'

Another doctor, asked how he felt after his first case of euthanasia, said simply, 'Awful'.

Of course, these emotional responses could be described as simple squeamishness which all health professionals need to overcome in order to practise effectively. But I believe these expressions of discomfort point to a deep moral unease, to a sense of having violated a moral boundary. They point to the hidden order of the creation. When we assist in the killing of another human being, however compassionate and rational our motives might seem to be, we come up against the moral order of the universe, and we damage our own humanity.

The human family

In Christian thought, not only is each individual human life special, but we are all members of the human family. We are created to be in community.

We see this in the enormous lengths that our society goes to in order to prevent suicides. Why are brave police officers expected to try to save the life of a man attempting to jump from a bridge, for example? Why on earth do they bother? If he wants to die, surely we should let him? Why risk the lives of valuable citizens attempting to save someone who doesn't value his own life?

I would suggest it is because our society, though penetrated by liberal individualism, is still deeply influenced by Christian intuitions. From a Christian perspective, we are not autonomous individuals doing our own thing. We are locked together in community, bound together by duties of care, responsibility and compassion. Respect for life, and the prohibition of suicide, is part of the glue that binds society together. It is part of the hidden moral order, the grain in the wood, which God has placed in the creation.

Respect for life, and the prohibition of suicide, is part of the glue that binds society together.

Imagine a society which quietly encouraged the depressed, the inadequate, the isolated or the disabled to take their own lives. Where doctors made available lethal mixtures for their patients, where the desperate and lonely were encouraged to get on with it. What kind of society would that be?

Instead, here is a Christian view of society, expressed in the well-known words of John Donne:

> No man is an island, entire of itself; every man is a piece of the continent, a part of the main. If a clod be washed away

by the sea, Europe is the less, as well as if a promontory were
. . . any man's death diminishes me, because I am involved in
mankind, and therefore never send to know for whom the
bell tolls; it tolls for thee.

It is because we are locked together in human community
that suicide can have devastating effects on others. Although
driven by desperation and hopelessness, the one who commits
suicide hurts those who survive. Whether intentionally or not,
the suicide strikes at all those in community with him or her,
wounding and damaging them, often for life.

The Dutch father of a Christian friend of mine rang up one
day to announce that he was going to receive euthanasia from
his doctor. Although not terminally ill, he was lonely and in
some pain. My friend had travelled to the Netherlands with his
own son to plead with his father not to do this. But his father
was adamant, and euthanasia was duly carried out the following
week. Now the family have to live the rest of their lives with a
sense of loss created by the actions of a loved family member.

When my loved one chooses to kill themselves rather than
carry on living with me, they point at my own inadequacies.
Perhaps I didn't love them enough. Perhaps I could have done
more. It is common to see this in cases of assisted suicide
reported in the media. In fact, at times there seems to be a
degree of emotional blackmail exerted by the suicidal individual: 'If you really loved me, you would help me to kill
myself.' The relatives often find themselves torn between
horror at the implications of suicide, loyalty to their loved
ones, and a deep sense of their own failure.

In summary, to commit suicide is to strike at the heart of
what it means to live in community, for we are designed to be
dependent on one another. We are all called to share the
burdens of the physical life which God has given us.

Death: an outrage and a mercy

I am struck by a curious ambivalence in orthodox Christian attitudes towards death. On the one hand, death is seen as an enemy and an outrage, and yet it can also be a mercy, a release, even a strange kind of healing. So because death is a terrible enemy, we are called to fight against it with all our courage, skill and commitment. Christian love is a way of saying to another person, even in the face of pain, suffering and disability, 'It is good that you are alive.' And in the resurrection of Jesus Christ we see the first-fruits of the ultimate defeat of death.

But in God's providential care for fallen human beings, death may become, in C. S. Lewis's phrase, 'a severe mercy'. In the biblical narrative, human lifespan is limited, not just as a curse, but out of God's grace. To live for ever in a fallen and decaying body is not a blessing, but a curse. In God's providence, death may be a merciful release from an existence trapped in a disintegrating body. So Christian attitudes to death must always reflect this strange ambiguity. Even though human death is fundamentally an evil to be fought against, a reality that can never be sought intentionally, it may also at times be accepted and recognized as a sign of God's mercy.

The person of Jesus

The Christian faith makes the astonishing claim that God has revealed himself in the physical stuff of our world, in a human person, Jesus of Nazareth. And the Gospel writers claimed that he rose physically from the grave on that first Easter Sunday. This shows us the importance of our current physical bodies, and also points to something that is even more important: the future resurrection life which is invading the present. The risen Jesus shows us that our present limited physical existence is not the only, or even the most important, part of reality. So Christians affirm the importance of physical healing, while recognizing that behind our current physical experience there lies a deeper, richer, even more wonderful reality.

This means that we cannot make the extension of physical life by technology the ultimate goal of medicine. Sometimes we have to say no to medical progress. Sometimes we shall need the trust and the courage that enable us to decline what medical technology makes possible. To say no to burdensome or futile medical treatment is not a form of suicide or faithlessness; it is part of wise Christian living. This physical existence is not all there is; we need a deeper healing.

In the next chapter we will look in more detail at decision-making on medical treatments at the end of life, but first we should revisit the deep mystery and reality of human suffering.

Human suffering: a mystery of human dependence

As we saw earlier, one of the novel features of our modern technological society is that we have lost the belief that suffering can have any positive value at all. Pain, whether physical, mental, relational or spiritual, is seen as useless, futile, destructive, incomprehensible and terrifying. It is the ultimate threat to individual human autonomy and self-direction. Once we have adopted this perspective, it is then an easy step to accept that, in the name of eliminating the suffering, we are forced to eliminate the sufferer.

Yet, within a Christian understanding, suffering can never be meaningless, even if it seems to be. Suffering is a painful reality that we are called to accept from the hand of a loving God. Even the word 'to suffer' implies an element of passivity.

It comes from the Latin *suffere*, meaning literally 'to bear under', and hence 'to permit or to allow'. The original meaning of the English word was 'to put up with', and hence the root meaning of suffering is the idea of submitting or being forced to submit or endure some circumstance which is beyond our control.

It seems this is the fundamental reason why suffering is regarded by secular philosophers as an affront to liberal ideas of individual autonomy. It is not so much that suffering impairs our ability to choose, but rather that suffering threatens the comforting illusion that we are in ultimate control. Suffering challenges our modern tendency to be control freaks. It challenges the widespread fantasy that we can be autonomous, choosing individuals. Instead, suffering emphasizes our deep and inescapable creaturely dependence. The suffering person cannot escape the reality of his or her profound dependence on others.

> '*Suffering is not a question which demands an answer, it is not a problem which demands a solution, it is a mystery which demands a presence.*'

As theologian Stanley Hauerwas has pointed out, the initial reaction to witnessing suffering in another human being is often to be repelled. Suffering tends to turn the other person into a stranger. Yet suffering in another human being is a call to the rest of us to stand in community. It is a call to be there. 'Suffering is not a question which demands an answer, it is not a problem which demands a solution, it is a mystery which demands a presence.'

So those of us who are called to care for suffering people need to encourage them, and demonstrate by our actions that they are not excluded from the human community. In fact, by providing committed and sensitive caring for suffering people, we are binding them into the human family. The sad reality is that, so often, modern medical and healthcare systems have precisely the opposite effect. They isolate and marginalize those who are suffering and dying from the rest of the human community.

The duty of care that doctors and other professional carers are bound by is a moral commitment to *be there* for those who are suffering and dying. It is a practical demonstration of the covenant bonds of community. It is to say to the sufferer, 'We are the community's representatives, and we promise to care for you whatever will happen, whatever it may cost. We will walk this road with you to the end.'

Of course, this does not mean that we ought to welcome or enjoy suffering. Orthodox Christian thinking has often been accused of masochism and callousness. But this is a perversion of what Christians have thought and practised over the centuries. Suffering is not to be sought, but there are times when it should, at least to some degree, be accepted.

Suffering and glory are inextricably linked

However, the Christian faith teaches us something more wonderful and mysterious than just the acceptance of suffering. In the biblical narrative, suffering and glory are inextricably linked and intertwined. The suffering Christ is also the glorified one. And there are mysterious hints in the New Testament that in the painful experience of suffering we may discover a profound intimacy with others who suffer, and with God himself:

I want to know Christ – yes, to know the power of his
resurrection and the participation [*koinonia*] in his sufferings,
becoming like him in his death.

(Philippians 3:10, NIV)

Blessed be the God and Father of our Lord Jesus Christ,
the Father of mercies and God of all comfort, who comforts
us in all our affliction, so that we may be able to comfort
those who are in any affliction, with the comfort with
which we ourselves are comforted by God. For as we share
abundantly in Christ's sufferings, so through Christ we
share abundantly in comfort too.

(2 Corinthians 1:3–5)

These are deep and complex topics, and this is not the place
to address them further. But in place of a simplistic utilitarian
philosophy that sees suffering and pain as entirely negative
and evil, the Christian faith provides a richer and more
nuanced understanding. Suffering need not be all loss. It is a
painful mystery that calls us to be a presence, to stand in
community with those in pain, to enter into the *koinonia* of
suffering.

We will now turn out attention to the practical medical
alternatives to assisted suicide and euthanasia.

8

Medical issues in the care of the dying person

It's all very well to argue that assisting suicide is not the best way to help dying people, but what does this mean in practice? How can we treat dying people with genuine compassion and with respect for their dignity and humanity? Is it ever right to say 'enough is enough' to medical treatment, or should we try to sustain life for as long as possible by giving every possible treatment?

We will now look at some real-world medical issues, asking how a Christian understanding of what it means to be human can be translated into practical caring.

Individual responses to imminent death

Over the years I have been struck by the differences in the responses of individuals as they face their imminent death, including those who have a strong Christian faith and hope of resurrection and future life. Some are very clear that they do not want invasive and burdensome treatment, and express their wishes for pain relief and symptom control only. They seem ready to move on to the next stage of existence. Others wish to cling to this life, whatever the cost in discomfort and distress. They insist on exploring every possible treatment option; they refuse to give up and they fight on to the end. Who are we to say which is better?

I have also come to realize that none of us can know how we ourselves will react until we face the reality of a terminal diagnosis. As individual moral agents, God gives us the freedom to make wise choices about our own lives, and we must respect that freedom in others, even if we would not make the same choices ourselves.

The problem of medical overtreatment

One of the driving forces for the legalization of euthanasia and assisted suicide is a type of medical overtreatment that doesn't respect the limits of our human abilities to treat disease. There seem to be many factors behind the epidemic of medical overtreatment in rich countries. Sometimes it is driven by medical arrogance and machismo, sometimes by perverse incentives that reward futile and burdensome treatments. Frequently it seems to be driven by medical inexperience or by fear of litigation. Even very experienced doctors may persist with overtreatment because of a sense that death represents failure and proves that the doctor was not good enough to keep the patient alive. It is not unusual for well-meaning relatives to compound the problem by insisting on every possible treatment as death approaches, whatever the consequences for their loved one.

Over the last few decades we have increasingly medicalized death and the process of dying. Death has become something that happens in hospitals, when the medical struggle against disease is finally lost. Dying has become a medical event.

Death is what happens when the doctors run out of treatment options. You keep going for as long as possible. You have every treatment that's available, but when you run out of treatment options, and when the doctors say, 'We are very sorry, but we have no other treatments left', then you die. Death becomes defined by what doctors can and cannot do.

Religious people often demand futile and burdensome treatment

In 2009 a study of 345 patients with advanced and terminal cancer was carried out in the USA. The researchers assessed each patient's attitude to death and the extent to which religion was important to them in coping with their illness. The researchers then followed every patient over the last year of life until death. Paradoxically, they found that 'religious coping behaviour' was associated with a markedly *increased* preference for receiving all possible medical measures, and lower rates of making a 'Do Not Resuscitate' statement, or completing an advance refusal of treatment, 'a living will'. In the last week of life people with religious coping behaviour were more likely to die in an intensive care unit receiving full life support to the very end, compared with the others.

Why was this? The researchers found that religious people said that they believed that only God could decide when a patient should die, and hence refusal of any possible treatment was 'tantamount to euthanasia'. Others said they believed they had to carry on with maximal treatment in case God was going to do a miracle. Some said that accepting palliative care meant 'giving up on God'. These results suggest that many believers think that they must have all possible treatments to the very end.

But it seems to me that these attitudes may reflect a deep-seated fear of death, a psychological denial of its inevitability and a desperate desire to use medical technology to hold death at bay for as long as possible, whatever the personal consequences. The temptation for modern doctors is to collude with this fear and denial of mortality and to use powerful and invasive technology in an inappropriate and harmful manner.

Recognizing the limits that come from our human nature

But doctors and health professionals, above all, must recognize the limitations of their technology and their abilities. This means that there are limits to what doctors can and should do in the quest for healing and the preservation of life. In fact, it can be argued that one of the primary roles of medical professionals in our society is to teach people the limits that come from our physical nature.

This is what theologian Stanley Hauerwas has called 'the wisdom of the body'. Disease provides an opportunity for learning more about the givenness and limitations of our physical nature.

> Medicine can be viewed as an educational process for both doctor and patient, in which each is both teacher and learner. It is from patients that physicians learn the wisdom of the body. Both physicians and patients must learn that each of them is subject to a prior authority – the authority of the body . . . medicine represents a way of learning to live with finitude.

At the heart of all decision-making about medical treatments is the balancing of the likely benefits of treatment against its burdens and risks. Good medical care has always included the withholding or withdrawing of treatment that is excessively burdensome relative to its likely benefits. This means that the weighing up of burdens and benefits of possible treatments is critically important – something that should be undertaken jointly and collaboratively by doctors, patients and their relatives.

Here is an individual with advanced bowel cancer. Is the burden of chemotherapy treatment, with all its unpleasantness, complications, risks, hospital visits, tests and expense, worth the benefits of increasing the chances of, maybe, a few extra weeks or months of survival? The answer is: 'It all depends.' In different circumstances, and with different individuals, the balance between burdens and benefits will change.

In some situations those extra weeks that invasive treatment can bring may be of profound significance and richness, an opportunity for all kinds of 'unfinished business' to be completed; the fulfilment of a long-cherished ambition, or the chance to enjoy the presence of children or intimate friends. In other situations those three months may seem to bring little benefit compared to the burdens, upset and complications of invasive treatment. It is all too possible for medical technology to transform the last weeks of life from a time of peaceful preparation for death into a living hell for all concerned.

Good medicine recognizes the difference between intention and foresight

The pro-euthanasia lobby ridicule the traditional view that doctors may give a drug to relieve suffering that may incidentally shorten life, but may not deliberately give a lethal medicine to end life. In their view, this is deeply hypocritical. They argue that doctors are in reality intending to kill with pain-killing medicines, but they mask their activities in order to avoid prosecution. This is supported by the misleading argument that morphine is a highly dangerous and lethal poison, and that when doctors give morphine at the end of life they are intending to kill but covering their tracks.

This is dangerous misinformation. Morphine and other opioids are highly effective painkillers, but in fact they are not dangerous lethal drugs, unless used in massive overdose. When doctors in the Netherlands and elsewhere intend to kill, directly or by assisting suicide, they do not use morphine. As we have seen, they use completely different drugs – barbiturates (in massive overdose) and muscle relaxants. These are the drugs of the anaesthetist, capable of inducing rapid-onset coma and muscle paralysis, not the drugs of palliative care doctors. The misinformation about morphine is dangerous, because patients may refuse to take adequate amounts of opioids for pain relief, fearing that the doctor is secretly trying to end their lives. In reality, there is good scientific evidence that when used appropriately in terminal illness, morphine and other opioids do not accelerate death, but paradoxically they sometimes extend life, as once pain and distress are controlled effectively, patients frequently regain the will to live.

Nevertheless, good medicine recognizes the difference between intention and foresight. This is the so-called 'principle of double effect'. This principle is often caricatured by opponents as an obscure form of 'Jesuitical' reasoning which is irrelevant to everyday life. In reality, it is a very basic ethical principle of medical practice.

Since the time of Hippocrates, it has been recognized that virtually all medical treatments carry negative side effects. In some cases the latter can be extremely severe or life-threatening. The intention behind the initiation of a treatment, the prescription of a drug or the undertaking of a therapeutic procedure is to bring good to the patient – to restore to health, to oppose a pathological process, or to bring relief from unpleasant symptoms of disease. Good intentions are central to the practice of moral medicine, as was stressed by Hippocrates: 'If the love of man is present [*philanthrope*], then love of the art [*philotechne*] is also present.'

The Hippocratic medical tradition

Arguably, for the first time in the history of healing and healers, the Hippocratic medical tradition drew a clear distinction between medical interventions intended to heal and those intended to harm. The Hippocratic Oath stated, 'I will use treatment to help the sick according to my ability and judgment, but I will never use it to injure or wrong them.'

Medical historians have recognized that this was a significant break from the previous tradition in which the roles of the doctor and the sorcerer were frequently combined. Margaret Mead, the anthropologist, put it like this:

> For the first time in the history of humankind there was a complete separation between killing and curing. Throughout the primitive world the doctor and the sorcerer tended to be the same person. He with the power to kill had the power to cure. He who had the power to cure would also be able to kill . . . With the Greeks, the distinction was made clear. One profession was to be dedicated completely to life under all circumstances, regardless of rank, age, or intellect – the life of a slave, the life of the Emperor, the life of the immigrant, the life of the defective child.

This dedication to human life has marked the medical profession for 2,000 years. This is why physicians who were faithful to the Hippocratic ideal refused to act as frontline combatants tasked to kill enemy soldiers, refused to participate in judicial executions, refused to participate in the torture of prisoners, refused to use psychiatric drugs to sedate political dissidents and refused to transplant organs from executed criminals. Their commitment was to the protection and preservation of life. And so there is a terrible irony and confusion in the suggestion that of all the possible professions who might be enrolled in the practice of assisted suicide, it is doctors who should become the professional killers, using their skill and expertise to calculate lethal dosages and induce swift cardiac arrest at will.

In Hippocratic terms, the intention behind every medical treatment should be to bring benefit, to promote the good of the patient. But while the intention is to bring good, all experienced clinicians are well aware of the severe and even life-threatening risks that some treatments bring. In my own medical practice I am sorry to say that some of the treatments I prescribed in good faith, and with good intentions, turned out to have devastating and even fatal side effects.

Of course, it is possible to give dangerous treatments with evil intent. It is possible for doctors to use medical interventions for homicidal purposes. This is the stuff of the medical whodunit paperback or horror movie. But I think we all share a deep moral intuition that distinguishes homicidal medical activities from the normal kind!

In the treatment of the dying patient my intention in withdrawing curative treatment is to relieve suffering, to bring benefit to the patient. I can foresee that my treatment decisions may shorten life, but that is not my intention.

The birth of palliative care

One of the most influential individuals in promoting effective pain relief at the end of life was Dame Cicely Saunders, whom we met earlier. She was an extraordinary person who pioneered a new way of caring for dying people that went round the world, and that remarkable initiative still reverberates today. Initially, she trained as a nurse, and then as a medical social worker in London in the 1940s. At that time traditional medical practice placed little emphasis on the care of dying people, who were often grossly neglected and abandoned in their last days and weeks.

Cicely was deeply moved by the experience of caring for a dying patient over the last two months of his life, and this experience became the touchstone for her life. She felt a deep sense of Christian vocation to devote her life to the care of the dying. At the age of thirty-three she enrolled as a medical student at St Thomas' Hospital in London and trained as a doctor. Her strong Christian faith was combined with a deeply compassionate nature, an innovative and creative approach to caring, and a steely determination to do the very best for her patients. After qualifying as a doctor and increasingly putting her radical ideas into practice, her work became focused on the creation of a new purpose-built hospice in South London, St Christopher's.

Dealing with 'total pain'

One of her most profound insights was the concept of 'total pain'. An elderly person was dying of cancer. There was gnawing and continuous *physical pain* because the cancer cells had invaded the bone. The physical pain was incessant, destructive and dehumanizing. But there was also mental or *psychological pain*, anxiety about what each day might bring. Often the fear of pain was as bad as the pain itself. There was despair and a sense of hopelessness at the recognition that life was coming to an end. Then there was *relational pain*, concerns about the effect of the cancer on a spouse or child. Perhaps there had been no contact with the oldest son for years, and now death was coming with no chance of reconciliation.

And finally, there was *spiritual pain*, maybe from feelings of unacknowledged guilt from past events, or a sense of the meaninglessness of existence. Cicely realized that each form of pain had to be addressed in order to maximize the well-being of the patient and, where possible, the family and relatives too, over the critical hours and days as death approached. She discovered that if anxiety, loneliness and spiritual pain were recognized and tackled, then very often the physical pain was much easier to control and alleviate.

Conversely, it is a common observation of palliative care doctors that when physical pain does not seem to respond, despite the administration of powerful medical treatments, it is highly likely that psychological, relational and spiritual factors are involved, and must be addressed. Many of the tragic high-profile cases of apparently 'uncontrollable pain' that are used by campaigners to promote the need for assisted suicide seem to be those where psychological, relational and spiritual factors dominated.

In order to tackle physical pain, Cicely Saunders used the latest pharmacological research evidence on pain-killing medication, together with meticulous observation and documentation from thousands of patients whom she and her colleagues had cared for. Using the expertise that they had accumulated, they demonstrated that it was possible for virtually all physical pain to be abolished, or at least substantially reduced, without causing extreme sedation and drowsiness. Her aim was that patients should be alert and able to respond to family, relatives and carers in the vital last days and hours of life.

Not just physical pain, but all unpleasant symptoms – nausea, itching, cough, dry mouth and so on – were to be addressed in minute detail with skilled nursing care. Psychological pain was tackled with human contact, friendship, music, humour, the encouragement of hobbies and interests, as well as professional counselling and support when necessary. Relational pain was approached by supporting and encouraging family members to be present, and welcoming openness and honest communication. And spiritual pain was addressed by placing prayer and worship at the centre of the community she was forming, inviting patients to celebrate Communion (often in beds and wheelchairs) in the chapel which was placed symbolically at the centre of St Christopher's.

Cicely stressed that St Christopher's would be open to patients of all faiths and of none, but hoped

> to render higher and more valuable service to our patients in their spiritual and mental than in their physical needs. These will . . . go hand in hand for faith in God is made infinitely easier by the faith in man which is created by the touch of kindness and the relief of pain and discomfort. Our Lord himself sent his disciples out both to heal and to teach; and work which combines both may have something of his own gracious presence. Though we cannot heal, there is a great deal that can be done to relieve the suffering of every dying person.

Dr Robert Twycross, another pioneer of the movement who had worked with Cicely Saunders, wrote, 'Palliative care developed as a reaction to the attitude, "There's nothing that can be done for you". This is never true. There's always something that can be done.'

Cicely pioneered an approach which put the dying person at the centre of care. Concern for the wishes and needs of each individual is at the heart. Pillows are arranged and re-arranged, the television is moved an inch or two until a comfortable position is found for the patient who cannot move his or her head. There is endless meticulous attention to mouth care, bathing sore eyes, putting cream on itchy skin, placing cushions between aching knees.

Being there

But above all, Cicely and her colleagues discovered that it is not primarily about doing things to patients – it is about 'being there' for each individual. Those words from the last chapter encapsulate her approach: 'Suffering is a mystery that demands a presence.' Through a number of intense and personal experiences of caring, she learned that

> it was possible to live a lifetime in a few weeks; that time is a matter of depth, not length; that in the right atmosphere and with pain controlled so that the patient is free to be herself, the last days can be the richest, they can be a time of reconciliation that makes the dying peaceful and the mourning bearable.

One of the best known of her sayings is: 'You matter because you are you, and you matter to the end of your life. We will do all we can not only to help you die peacefully, but also to live until you die.' 'To live until you die' became one of the slogans of a new kind of caring, and the foundation of the medical specialty of palliative care.

'You matter because you are you, and you matter to the end of your life.'

So Cicely Saunders and St Christopher's Hospice in South London became the hub of a movement that has spread out across the world. The philosophy and principles of palliative care were established and taught, research into pain relief and symptom control took off, and training programmes were established. Many other hospices were established, but increasingly, the principles and practices of palliative care were extended into the community, to help people dying at home, and into general hospital practice. What Cicely had founded was a concept, an approach to the individualized care of the whole person, much more than an institution.

She was strongly opposed to the legalization of euthanasia. In 1969, when an early Bill to legalize euthanasia was being debated in the House of Lords, she wrote to the *Times* newspaper, 'We, as doctors, are concerned to emphasize that there are few forms of physical distress which cannot be dealt with by good medical and nursing care, that the emotional and spiritual distress of incurable disease requires human understanding and compassion and a readiness to listen and help, rather than a lethal drug.'

Cicely's arguments against euthanasia and all forms of medical killing were put forward forcefully and simply. First, it is *unnecessary* – pain can nearly always be controlled and alleviated; the body and the mind can be made comfortable while the patient remains alert and fully themselves. 'You don't have to kill the patient in order to kill the pain.' Secondly, it is *dangerous* – 'any law permitting voluntary euthanasia pulls the rug from under the vulnerable.' Once euthanasia was made available, it would put pressure on the sick and the elderly, all too conscious of the demands they were putting on their relatives: 'To make voluntary euthanasia lawful would be an irresponsible act, hindering help, pressurising the vulnerable, abrogating our true respect and responsibility to the frail and old, the disabled and dying.'

There is no doubt that the powerful and attractive model of palliative care, which was increasingly spreading across the UK and then across the world, played a vital role in counteracting the legalization of euthanasia in the UK from the 1960s onwards. Some years ago I happened to be sitting next to an eminent medical member of the House of Lords who had been at the heart of debates about euthanasia for decades. I asked him why he thought that euthanasia had developed in the Netherlands from the 1960s, but had not been legalized in the UK despite numerous attempts. 'Oh, that's very simple,' he said. 'I can sum up the whole thing in two words: "Cicely Saunders".'

Why was this woman so convinced that euthanasia legislation would be dangerous? In the final section of this chapter we turn briefly to review the possible dangers and risks that legislation for assisted suicide might bring.

Risks of assisted suicide legislation

a. Wrong diagnosis
Sadly, serious mistakes in diagnosis are not uncommon, even in specialist centres. The last few years have seen a number of public scares, as major errors have been revealed in pathology laboratories responsible for the diagnosis of cancer. How likely is it that assisted suicide might be carried out in the mistaken belief that the patient was terminally ill, when in fact the disease was self-limiting? Assisted suicide legislation would open up more possibilities for serious medical mishaps.

b. Wrong prognosis
Even when doctors make the right diagnosis, they are frequently wrong as they attempt to predict how long a patient will survive. Most medical prognostication in terminal illness is more akin to educated guesswork than scientific calculation. Yet the proposed legislation assumes that a doctor can confidently predict both that the patient is terminally ill and that

death will occur naturally within an arbitrary period of six months. One high-profile example of inaccurate prognosis was the Lockerbie bomber Abdelbaset al-Megrahi who was freed from a Scottish prison in August 2009 on the grounds that he was about to die. Detailed medical reports by eminent UK specialists indicated that he had terminal prostate cancer and an estimated three months to live. In reality, he survived until May 2012, two years and nine months later.

c. Pressures on vulnerable people at the end of life

As Cicely Saunders argued (and as discussed earlier), the availability of assisted suicide and euthanasia would place implicit pressure on the sick and the elderly, all too conscious of the demands they put on their relatives. Although the proposed legislation states that the request should come from the patient, in the highly regulated nature of medical care in the UK, once assisted suicide legislation was enacted, it is likely that doctors would be instructed to make sure that all of their terminally ill patients were aware that it was an option. To fail to inform patients about the option of suicide, even if the doctor thought it was totally inappropriate, would open the possibility of the doctor being sued. Assisted suicide would be added to the list of 'treatment options'. How many vulnerable people would then perceive the option of medical suicide as a duty? If there is no possibility of life termination, then I do not need to justify my desire to continue living. But once life termination becomes a 'treatment option', then I need to provide some justification for my desire to continue to live.

d. Abuse by relatives

Proponents of assisted suicide dismiss the possibility that relatives might pressurize elderly and infirm people for their own gain. But in the real world inhabited by clinicians, social workers and law enforcement agencies this is sadly not unusual. There is the possibility of serious abuse by relatives, who might see assisted suicide as a legally approved opportunity to relieve themselves of a burden of caring, and preventing the dissipation of life savings on expensive nursing care. This is not to imply that most relatives harbour malevolent thoughts towards the terminally ill. But their own emotional distress can be a major source of pressure for health carers: 'I can't bear to watch her in this state. Why can't you give her something to end it all?' How long will it be before the 'right to die' becomes a 'duty to die'?

A palliative care consultant recalled the relatives of a dying person in her care who repeatedly expressed concerns that their mother's pain was not controlled. They continued to ask that pain relief and sedation should be increased, although the lady in question appeared settled and peaceful. Subsequently, it became apparent that there was an insurance policy in place, and that a substantial amount of money would be paid to the relatives if their mother died before a certain anniversary. Once the anniversary came and went, and the person was still alive, the relatives seemed to lose interest in the degree of pain control.

e. Accidental failure of suicide procedures
(This section is rather grisly, so those of a sensitive disposition are advised to skip to the next section.)
All doctors with experience of assisted suicide recognize that 'failures' will occur from time to time. In a study published in the *New England Journal of Medicine* complications occurred in 7% of cases of assisted suicide, and problems with completion (a longer-than-expected time to death, failure to induce coma, or induction of coma followed by the awakening of the patient) occurred in 16% of cases. The physician decided

to administer a lethal medication (intravenously) in 18% of the cases of assisted suicide because of problems with the procedure. The Royal Dutch Medical Association recommends that a doctor be present when assisted suicide is performed, precisely so that euthanasia can be performed, if necessary.

Following oral administration of large doses of barbiturates, there are reports of extreme gasping and muscle spasms. While losing consciousness, vomiting and aspiration may occur. Panic, feelings of terror and assaultive behaviour may take place from the drug-induced confusion. In one reported case in Oregon, after a man took the drugs intended to induce death, his physical symptoms were so disturbing that his wife called the emergency services. He was taken from his home to a hospital where he was revived.

A Dutch doctor with practical experience of both voluntary euthanasia and assisted suicide said,

> Thinking that physician-assisted suicide is the entire answer to the question of ending of life of a suffering patient . . . is a fantasy. There will always be patients who cannot drink, or are semiconscious, or prefer that a physician perform this act. Experience has taught us that there are many cases of assisted suicide in which the suicide fails. Physicians need to be aware of the necessity to intervene before patients awaken.

Yet the proposed UK legislation takes no account of the possibility of complications in the suicide procedure. Doctors would not be allowed to intervene by administering further lethal medication, even if severe aspiration and brain damage resulted from a botched suicide attempt. How long will it be before direct medical killing is seen as an acceptable response when suicide goes wrong?

f. Risks from the prescription and supply of lethal medications

The assisted-suicide procedure would require that doctors prescribe and supply to the patient highly lethal medication for his or her own use. The possibilities of errors, accidents and abuse are obvious.

The Falconer Commission stated,

> We are very concerned to avoid the potentially dangerous ramifications of allowing lethal medication to be kept in an unregulated manner in the community, in a private home, residential care home, hospice or hospital. We have suggested a number of safeguards that could ensure the lethal medication that would be required to bring about an assisted death was stored and transported safely. Most importantly, the doctor responsible for prescribing the lethal medication, or another suitably qualified healthcare professional, would be expected to deliver the medication to the patient personally and wait until the patient had either taken the medication or declined to take the medication. If the medication was unused, we recommend that it should be legally required that it is returned to the pharmacy.

Although this proposal seems well-meaning, the presence of the doctor or healthcare professional could provide subtle pressure for the patient to take the lethal medication so as not to waste the professional's valuable time.

g. Gradual and incremental extension of the grounds for assisted suicide

As discussed in chapter 5, the proposed grounds for assisted suicide are highly arbitrary and cannot be justified on rational grounds. Legislation in other countries has different time limits and criteria. Following enactment of the legislation, there would still be a steady stream of suffering and tragic individuals demanding the right to have an assisted suicide in the UK. Many of the high-profile media cases that have caused such public sympathy (including Daniel James, Tony Nicklinson and Sir Edward Downes) would not be eligible for assisted suicide under the proposed legislation. It is inevitable that media campaigns and legal challenges would continue, and it seems highly unlikely that the grounds for assisted suicide would remain unchanged.

h. Effects of assisted suicide on health professionals and on society as a whole

Although it is proposed that no doctor would be forced to participate in assisted suicide, as discussed above, it is likely that it would eventually become mandatory for all doctors to make their terminally ill patients aware that assisted suicide was an option. Would health professionals put as much emphasis on suicide prevention for the rest of their patients if assisted suicide was available for some of them? Would a minority of doctors who were strongly in favour of assisted suicide make their services widely available?

Finally, there is the effect on society of legalized medical killing, and the existence of a specialized group of people who are authorized to plan and assist killing under certain circumstances. Would suicide gradually become rehabilitated and promoted as a rational and reasonable way to die? Would the prevention of suicide come to be seen as paternalistic and outmoded? Respect for human life and resistance to suicide have been part of the glue that has bound our communities together for hundreds of years. Would legalized medical killing cheapen respect for human life in society as a whole?

In the next chapter we will look at recent developments in palliative medicine, the current legal framework for decisions at the end of life, and the challenges that need to be overcome in improving the medical and nursing care of dying people in hospital and at home.

9

Palliative care and legal frameworks

> You matter because you are you, and you matter to the end
> of your life. We will do all we can not only to help you die
> peacefully, but also to live until you die.
> (Cicely Saunders)

It is a strange paradox that here, in the twenty-first century, the expertise of pain specialists and the power of new pharmacological and other approaches to symptom control have never been greater. This is particularly true in the UK, which is internationally recognized as a world leader in pain control and palliative care. Yet despite these remarkable advances, as we have seen, the pressure to legalize medical killing in the UK and elsewhere has never been so urgent. This strongly suggests that the drive to change the law is based not so much on enlightenment and compassion for those who suffer (whatever the public rhetoric), as on the drive for autonomy, individualism and 'lifestyle choice'.

This chapter looks in more detail at the practice of palliative care as an alternative to assisted suicide, and then focuses on the current legal framework concerning medical and care decisions at the end of life.

Curative treatment and palliative medicine

Building on the pioneering work of Cicely Saunders and others, palliative medicine has developed a philosophy which separates it from most other forms of conventional medicine. The goals of conventional curative medical treatments can be summarized under three headings: the reversal of disease processes in order to ensure the preservation, protection and prolongation of life; the preservation and restoration of normal human functioning; and the relief of pain and other distressing and unwanted symptoms. In terms of priorities, in most medical treatment the preservation and protection of life comes first, and all other goals are subordinate.

Conventional medical treatment may also be subdivided into 'curative treatment', where the goal is to destroy completely disease processes within the body and restore the patient to health, and 'active medical treatment', where the goal is to alter the course of the disease, without bringing a permanent cure. For instance, in many forms of advanced cancer intensive chemotherapy can significantly prolong life, but cannot cure the disease completely.

Hospital doctors often refer to limitations of treatment or 'ceilings of care'. As discussed previously, the decision to give any treatment has to be made after weighing up the potential benefits against potential burdens and risks. As a person's disease progresses, the likelihood of benefitting from invasive treatment decreases, and the likelihood of side effects and complications increases. Clinicians may then determine (with the knowledge and agreement of the patient) that there should be a ceiling of care beyond which they will not go, in order to reduce the harm to a patient caused by overtreatment. Ceilings of care may include the decision not to commence cardiopulmonary resuscitation in the event of a cardiac arrest, if it is agreed that resuscitation would be unlikely to succeed and would deprive the individual of a peaceful death. A person with advanced disease may decide against being admitted to hospital, or against being transferred to an intensive care unit, accepting that he or she would rather receive palliative care and symptom control instead of the additional burdens imposed by invasive, uncomfortable and medically futile treatment.

The goals of palliative care

Palliative medical treatment is appropriate once it is clear that curative treatment is unlikely to bring any benefit. It has different goals and priorities compared with conventional medical treatment. Since death is now inevitable, the primary goal of all palliative treatment is the relief of pain and distressing symptoms. The aim of palliative care is neither to prolong life, to try to ensure that death is held back for as long as humanly possible, nor is it to deliberately shorten life, to hasten death and bring the end of life as rapidly as possible. Instead, the aim is to concentrate elsewhere – on the person's well-being and experience of life in the precious last days, weeks and months that may remain. To help people 'live before they die'.

More than half a century after Cicely Saunders started her revolution, palliative medicine is developing and rapidly advancing. Innovations and improvements in pain relief and symptom control continue to take place. From a medical perspective, symptom control in terminal cancer is usually very effective. But many more people are now dying from neurological conditions such as multiple sclerosis or chronic respiratory or cardiac failure, bringing new challenges to creative and skilled caring. Research into improved care for those with chronic neurological and cardiorespiratory conditions is now a major focus, and incremental advances in palliative techniques and interventions continue to take place.

End-of-life or terminal care

It is often helpful to distinguish palliative care, which may continue for many weeks, months and even years, from end-of-life or terminal care, which is an important subsection of palliative care. The latter is given to a person in the final hours of their life, a period usually covering anything from a few hours up to two to three days. During this phase the person may be described as 'actively dying'. The individual may be fully conscious or may move in and out of consciousness. Control of unpleasant symptoms is even more critical than previously, and the family may need a great deal of intensive support at this very difficult time. This kind of care is often delivered in a hospice or a person's own home, where possible, with detailed attention to the needs of the whole person – their physical and mental symptoms, their need for relationships and family support, and their spiritual needs. However, in some cases, particularly where there are complex symptoms, or a patient is not fit enough to be transferred and death is imminent, end-of-life care is best given in hospital.

Using a slow infusion of painkillers, anti-vomiting medication and mild but non-lethal sedatives, patients can remain comfortable without hastening death. With skilled care, many remain conscious and able to communicate without being in marked discomfort or distress. It is generally recognized that it is helpful to identify the terminal phase in which the patient is 'actively dying' so that unnecessary interventions can be stopped and appropriate care can be provided.

However, diagnosing when death is imminent is a far more imprecise science than many lay people realize, and accurate prediction of death in non-cancer patients is particularly difficult. The truth is that there are no very precise ways of telling accurately when a patient is in the last days of life. And it is not unusual for an individual who appears to have entered the final last hours of life to reverse his or her course and show some temporary improvement, sometimes for days, weeks or even longer. It is also undoubtedly true that the reaction of the individual to the approach of death may make a substantial difference. Some people show acceptance and equanimity, whereas others may fight to stave it off for as long as possible, perhaps because they wish to see a family anniversary, or other significant event.

It is important that relatives and carers understand that it is frequently impossible even for highly experienced health staff to predict the timing of death with any accuracy. As we saw earlier, death and dying have profound symbolic importance for us as moderns, because they challenge the comforting illusion that we are in control of our own lives or of the lives of those close to us. Walking with a dying person to the end reminds us forcefully that we are fragile, limited and dependent beings.

Attitudes of palliative care specialists to euthanasia and assisted suicide

The great majority of specialists in palliative medicine have remained strongly opposed to the legalization of euthanasia and assisted suicide. In a 2015 survey of specialists from the UK Association of Palliative Medicine, 82% opposed a change in the law on assisted suicide. Another recent survey by the Royal College of Physicians found that 92% of palliative care physicians opposed medically assisted suicide. It is striking that those with the greatest practical experience of caring for dying people are also those who are most strongly opposed to it.

One prominent example is Baroness Illora Finlay, Professor of Palliative Medicine at Cardiff University, who is an active campaigner against the legalization of assisted suicide. She stresses the remarkable advances that have been made in pain and symptom control since she started work in the 1970s. Experienced practitioners like Baroness Finlay observe that terminally ill patients frequently experience feelings of hopelessness, despair and depression, and at that moment death may seem the obvious way out. The patient may ask in desperation why the doctor doesn't just kill them to end it all. But carers learn to identify and address 'the question behind the question': 'Why me?', 'Why now?', 'Why does no-one seem to care?' The request to be killed may in fact be an expression of fear, hopelessness or despair, and to the experienced and compassionate carer it offers an opportunity for deeper understanding, engagement and support.

Communicating honestly with the healthcare team and with loved ones

As the terminal phase of life approaches, there are important topics that may need to be discussed with the medical team, family and care-givers:

Are there important things I want to accomplish before I die? Are there people to see, relationships to restore, affairs to set in order? Dying offers an opportunity for priorities to be changed, and some people find an intensity of purpose despite physical frailty and fatigue.

What symptoms am I likely to suffer, and how can these be reduced? Talking to professionals in advance can provide reassurance about the range of treatments that are available to ensure that unpleasant symptoms are well controlled. Being honest about our fears and anxieties can help the healthcare team to ensure that our particular concerns are addressed.

Where would I like to die? Although in reality many people die in hospital, most people when asked would prefer to die at home, or in a hospice. Community palliative care teams exist to provide excellent end-of-life care in a variety of settings.

Who will support me spiritually? Good palliative care aims to support the whole person, and to address all forms of distress – physical, psychological and spiritual. Maintaining good pastoral care from friends at church, or from a trusted pastor or elder, may be of vital importance in sustaining Christian faith as death approaches. We are not alone in the Christian family, and we are called to bear one another's burdens, to be there for one another and to say to each one, 'It's good that you are alive.'

Making palliative care widely available

Only about 10% of all deaths in the UK occur in specialist hospices. The majority of people die in an NHS hospital. Outside the UK, hospice care is even more uncommon. The task has been to take the very best care practices and techniques developed in the hospices, and make them widely available in general hospitals and in the care of people dying at home.

But this has proved problematic and challenging. High-quality palliative care is not technologically sophisticated, but it does not come easily or cheaply. It requires a skilled, experienced and motivated multidisciplinary team available around the clock. The Liverpool Care Pathway (LCP) was a UK initiative to translate the best practices of palliative care developed in hospices into a form suitable for staff without specialist palliative care experience working in an NHS general hospital. The LCP was originally developed by the Royal Liverpool University Hospital and the Marie Curie Hospice in Liverpool for the care of terminally ill cancer patients. Sadly, this well-meaning initiative led to many highly publicized instances of poor care, failures of communication between staff and relatives, and accusations that staff were using the LCP protocol inappropriately to hasten death.

In 2013 an official review panel was set up into the working of the LCP, and a report was published entitled 'More Care, Less Pathway'. The panel concluded that the LCP was not being applied properly in many cases, and that generic protocols were the wrong approach. It was recommended that use of the LCP should be replaced by an end-of-life care plan for each patient, together with good practice guidance for the patient's specific condition. (See more about this in Appendix 4, which also contains a discussion of two aspects of the medical care of dying patients that have aroused particular concern and controversy: the provision of fluids and nutrition, and the topic of terminal sedation.)

The controversies around the provision of palliative care highlight the fact that people often have specific and widely differing concerns about the care they will receive when they are close to death. One commonly expressed concern is that the individual may be neglected and abandoned as death approaches, and that hospital staff may covertly attempt to ensure that he or she dies rapidly, by withdrawing fluids and giving excessive doses of sedation. These understandable concerns have led people to insist that they receive active medical treatment up to the end of life, together with clinically assisted nutrition and hydration (that is, food and fluids that are given by a tube – usually directly into the stomach).

However, the opposite concern is also frequently expressed, namely that the doctors will attempt to keep the individual alive far too long, using painful and distressing invasive treatments, instead of allowing death to occur from natural causes. These understandable concerns have led people to insist that they should not receive life-sustaining or active medical treatment if it can bring no benefit, and that clinically assisted nutrition or hydration should not be given in the terminal phase.

In summary, every individual is different, and good palliative and end-of-life care must be highly sensitive and responsive to the wishes of the individual and his or her family.

Can we afford to provide palliative care for everyone who needs it?

As stated above, good-quality palliative care is not cheap. An authoritative independent review in 2011 found that over 450,000 people in the UK needed good palliative care services every year, and over 90,000 per year were not receiving proper care. However, the same review found that providing appropriate palliative care in the community across the UK, enabling those who wished to die at home to do so, would be overall cost-neutral for the state. This is because the cost of dying in hospital is considerably greater than dying at home with appropriate professional support and care.

It was estimated that the NHS spent 460 million pounds on palliative care in 2011. This is a large sum, but it represents considerably less than 1% of the NHS total budget per year. As a country, we put vastly more resources into research into finding new treatments for cancer and other means of extending life than we do into providing good palliative care for everyone who needs it. So there is no doubt that we, and all those in developed countries, can afford this kind of care. The issue is one of priorities for allocating healthcare resources. Sadly, providing good palliative care in poor countries which can allocate only a few dollars per person per year for healthcare is a major challenge, but there has been remarkable progress recently in the provision of palliative care in low-resource countries through charities and non-governmental organizations (NGOs).

Current legal framework for end-of-life decisions

This section focuses on the current legal framework in England and Wales, although similar legislation is now in force in many jurisdictions. The bedrock of current medical law is that all decisions about medical treatments must be taken in the patient's best interests, and that if the patient has legal capacity to decide on their own treatment, then he or she must give their free and informed consent to all treatment. If a patient with capacity refuses treatment, then the doctors must respect that refusal, even if it leads to the shortening of life. If the patient has capacity, then the next of kin and other relatives have no legally binding right to be involved in treatment decisions, although of course the patient may wish them to be involved.

In England and Wales the Mental Capacity Act governs the care which is provided to adults who lack capacity to make decisions on their own behalf. The fundamental principle is that all care must be provided in the individual's 'best interests' and in a way that causes the least restriction on his or her rights and freedom of action.

According to the Act, every adult is presumed to have capacity to make decisions on any matter unless it has been determined that they lack capacity. The law also recognizes that each person may have capacity to make some decisions but not others. In other words, you may have the legal capacity to make a relatively minor decision, but not one with serious and irreversible consequences. All reasonable steps must be taken to enable you to make your own decisions, including ensuring that the information is presented in a way that you can easily understand. With regard to the care of the dying patient, if the medical team conclude that the patient lacks capacity, then it is their duty to make treatment decisions based on the best interests of the patient.

The Mental Capacity Act sets out the steps that should be taken to determine a person's best interests. This will include consideration of:

a. their past and present wishes and feelings (and in particular, any relevant written statement made when they had capacity);
b. the beliefs and values that would be likely to influence their decision if they had capacity;
c. any other factors that you would be likely to consider.

In addition, the Act states that the doctors should take account of the views of relatives, any person who was previously named for that purpose, anyone engaged in caring for the person, and any named individual with a Lasting Power of Attorney (see below).

Many relatives mistakenly believe that they have the legal right or duty to make medical decisions on behalf of the individual who is dying. However, this is not correct. If the dying person still has legal capacity, then it is entirely up to that individual to what extent relatives and carers should be involved. If the person loses capacity, then, under the Mental

Capacity Act, the legal responsibility for treatment decisions rests with the treating doctors (and particularly with the doctor who carries overall responsibility for his or her care – in hospital practice this is a named consultant). However, the medical team do have a duty to consult the next of kin, and other relatives and carers, as part of the process laid down by the Act in determining the best interests of the patient.

Under the Mental Capacity Act there are two main ways for a person to make preparations in advance to help with decision-making at the end of life, when he or she may have lost capacity.

Lasting Power of Attorney

The first option is to create a Health and Welfare Lasting Power of Attorney (LPA). This involves signing a formal document that appoints one or more named individuals to make decisions on your behalf, if and when you lose capacity. The LPA may be given to a spouse, a close adult relative, a close friend or to a solicitor. If you appoint more than one attorney, they can be appointed either so that they must act together or so that they can act separately. You can also appoint replacements if the primary attorney(s) become(s) unable to act. The LPA only comes into force once you have lost capacity, and the LPA has been registered with the Office of the Public Guardian (OPG).

Health and welfare LPAs cover decisions including accommodation, care and all aspects of day-to-day living, as well as decisions on medical matters. If you wish, you can give your attorneys authority to give or refuse consent to life-sustaining treatment, on your behalf. The medical team will be legally bound to follow your attorneys' decisions. The attorneys have a legal responsibility to act in the person's best interests. Not surprisingly, under current English and Scottish law, an LPA does not give legal right to an attorney to authorize euthanasia or assisted suicide of the individual concerned – such acts are illegal. Registration of an LPA with the Office of the Public Guardian takes about three months, and so advance planning is necessary. An LPA can be made, revoked or updated at any time, so long as you still have mental capacity to do so.

An Advance Decision

The alternative mechanism laid down in the Mental Capacity Act is a legally binding document called an Advance Decision. This is sometimes referred to as a 'living will'. It is an expression of the person's wishes about future treatment, or about some other aspect of his or her general health and welfare that may arise in the future.

The main value of an Advance Decision is to *refuse consent* to a particular treatment. It is not possible legally to demand any particular treatment, but it is possible to refuse consent in advance, including refusal of life-supporting treatment. If the Advance Decision relates to life-supporting treatment, it must be in writing and signed by the person in the presence of a witness who must also sign the document. There is no form of prescribed wording, but clearly the more precise the better.

At some future time, if the person is admitted to hospital with a life-threatening illness, the medical team will need to decide whether the Advance Decision is valid. In particular, they will need to determine that the Advance Decision relates to the particular circumstances and treatment(s) which are being considered. They will also need to check that the person has not subsequently withdrawn the decision, and that he or she has not behaved subsequently in a way that is clearly inconsistent with it.

What are the advantages and disadvantages of the above?
The Advance Decision is much more straightforward to set up, and there are fewer formalities involved. However, in reality, it may be much less useful than initially appears. It is very hard to predict in advance the precise clinical circumstances that may occur months or years later, when you may be admitted to hospital in an incapacitated form. As a result, the Advance Decision may turn out to be invalid in practice, because it does not deal with the precise treatments or conditions that are being considered by doctors.

Alternatively, it might be argued by doctors or relatives that the person had changed his or her mind following the writing of the document. There is also the possibility that an Advance Decision may have unforeseen consequences. For instance, an elderly person with a life-limiting condition might write an Advance Decision giving a blanket refusal to any form of life-support treatment. However, this might mean that doctors would fail to give intensive treatment for an incidental treatable condition such as pneumonia, even though treatment might well have given a good chance of prolonging reasonably healthy survival by many months.

The LPA by comparison is legally more robust and covers a very wide range of possibilities. Your attorneys are given legal power to act on your behalf, including in circumstances that you had not imagined in advance, provided that they always act in what they believe are your best interests. This means they must take account of your past and present feelings and beliefs. As a result, it is very valuable to write a separate document which sets out your wishes, beliefs and values regarding medical treatment and care at the end of your life. This document which states your wishes can be updated as you see fit. (See below for more detailed discussion about this form of statement.)

The LPA gives very wide legal powers to the attorney. This may create a level of responsibility which some may see as burdensome. For instance, you may wish to nominate a spouse or grown-up son or daughter as your attorney. Months or years later it is possible that you are admitted to hospital in an unconscious state, and an acute life-threatening illness is diagnosed. If it is covered under the wording of the LPA, then your loved one carries strong legally binding powers to give consent, or to refuse life-sustaining treatment on your behalf. The doctors will almost certainly be bound to follow your attorney's decisions. This means that your loved one must carry responsibility for life-and-death decisions on your behalf, and they must live with the consequences of those decisions for the rest of their lives.

A written statement of wishes and values

The Mental Capacity Act specifically makes provision for a person to write a statement of their wishes, feelings and values while they still have capacity. This written statement must be taken into account by the medical teams, by attorneys, and by any others who have to determine the individual's best interests once he or she has lost capacity. Although this document is not legally binding, it can be extremely useful for everyone involved. It can be particularly helpful to express your own individual values, concerns and desires about the end of your life.

There is no specific format that the statement should take. It would obviously be helpful to include family members in discussions about the content, to minimize the possibility of uncertainty or disagreement about implementing your wishes. It is also important to keep any statement up to date and to make sure that copies are given to family members, people holding an LPA, the GP, and other doctors and carers who may be involved. It is obviously essential that important people in your life are aware of the document. Another practical tip might be to carry a card in your wallet or handbag, so that people can be directed to where they can find the relevant document(s) in the event of an unforeseen accident or health issue.

In creating a statement of wishes and values, as with an Advance Decision, it is not possible to demand that specific treatments will be given. Medical teams are not obliged to start, or to continue, medical treatments if they consider them to be against a patient's best interests, and this includes artificial hydration and nutrition.

However, if you are concerned that treatments may be withdrawn inappropriately, for instance in the case of a person with chronic disabilities who worries that doctors might consider that his or her life was no longer worth living, then it is possible to record these concerns as part of a statement of wishes. For example, it would be possible to state that you wish to be provided with clinically assisted nutrition and/or hydration where these have a reasonable chance of sustaining your life or easing your symptoms.

You will find a sample Statement of Wishes and Values, written for a Christian believer facing a life-limiting illness, in Appendix 1.

To conclude, good palliative care allows people to die at peace, and with dignity, and (just as importantly) it enables them to live before they die. But, as so often, the right way is not necessarily an easy way. We have seen that there may be complex technical, legal and personal issues that must be addressed if the very best level of medical, nursing and personal care is to be provided in the last weeks, days and hours of life. Perhaps of greatest importance is the need to start a conversation with our closest relatives and friends, in advance of the crisis. (The end of the book provides a list of resources and materials that may be helpful.)

In the final chapter we will summarize the conclusions we have reached, and reflect briefly on what it means to die well and in a manner that is consistent with the Christian faith.

10

Dying well and dying faithfully

I am conscious that we have covered a lot of ground in a few pages, and that it is possible to lose the big picture in a mass of complex details. In this final chapter I will try to stand back – to review and summarize the main arguments and debates from previous chapters – before briefly turning to a distinctively Christian understanding of what it means to die well. If you wish to skip the summary, please turn on to the next heading, 'Dying well in the light of the future' (page 155). In a subsequent book I hope to address in greater detail some of the personal and pastoral issues: dying well in the light of the hope of the resurrection; dying in a manner consistent with the Christian faith.

Surveying the journey

We started with the public profile of a small number of highly motivated individuals who demanded the right to kill themselves. The number of British people who travel to Switzerland to commit suicide is tiny, but they represent the tip of an iceberg – one of the pieces of evidence that profound changes are occurring in attitudes towards suicide and medical killing.

In chapter 2 we looked at the tragic, confusing and downright bizarre history of medical killing. We noted the persistent connection between interest in euthanasia and the development of 'scientific' eugenics in Victorian Britain. Proposals for euthanasia in the UK in the 1930s were comparable to those of Binding and Hoche in Germany that were subsequently adopted by the Third Reich. As the unspeakable horrors of the Nazi euthanasia programme emerged into public view after the end of the Second World War, it is not surprising that the UK euthanasia movement sought to distance itself, but the similarities between UK and German thinking about euthanasia and eugenics in the pre-war period are undeniable.

The development of voluntary euthanasia in the Netherlands was formulated for those with 'unbearable and hopeless suffering', focusing on the doctor's duty to relieve suffering. In 2002 the Netherlands became the first country in the world to legalize both euthanasia and medically assisted suicide, and some form of medical killing (usually lethal injection) has become almost routine where there is advanced terminal disease. In addition, many more die from the increasingly common practice of terminal sedation, although this is not recognized as intentional hastening of death by many Dutch doctors.

There seems to be strong pressure from the lay public for Dutch doctors to modify their clinical practice by extending euthanasia to patients with dementia and those deemed to be suffering unbearably from psychiatric illness. There is also pressure to provide euthanasia for elderly individuals who are 'tired of life', although the Dutch medical organization remains strongly opposed to this at the time of writing.

Some people argue that the Dutch experience demonstrates the value of a well-regulated euthanasia practice which is open to legal and public scrutiny. But the evidence of a gradual progression and extension in medical termination of life, and of increasing pressures on doctors to comply with social demands for medicalized death, seems incontrovertible.

Oregon represents a very different approach, in that only assisted suicide with oral drugs is allowed, no requirement exists for any suffering to have been identified, but a diagnosis of a terminal illness is essential. Although Oregon is often presented as a model for future UK practice, in reality there is a remarkably lax reporting system, based entirely on trust. There is no specific regulatory authority, and the apparent lack of complications from the ingestion of lethal drugs seems directly inconsistent with the experience of doctors in the Netherlands. Belgium and Switzerland represent further variations in assisted suicide and euthanasia practice, with Belgium having recently extended euthanasia to children of any age.

In summary, the international perspective indicates that there is no consistency in the practice of legally sanctioned euthanasia and assisted suicide, and that many of the approaches adopted around the world are mutually contradictory.

In chapter 3 we looked at the UK approach – that of distancing itself from Netherlands-style euthanasia in favour of Oregon-style assisted suicide. It is argued that proposed legalization will be limited to 'assisting the dying' of a small number of terminally ill individuals who wish to end their lives. However, in private, many campaigners concede that the proposed law will not satisfy the highly publicized needs of those who are very severely disabled and unable to commit suicide, nor those who wish to die but are not terminally ill. Many, such as Baroness Mary Warnock, regard the legalization of assisted suicide as the first step towards more wide-reaching liberalization of the law to allow suicide and mercy killing in a range of circumstances.

To many, the use of the benign phrase 'assisted dying' seems deliberately intended to mislead. In reality, what is being proposed is intentional termination of life. The doctor has to agree with the patient that his or her life is not worth living, and calculates the lethal dosage and provides advice and support for the killing process – but the doctor hangs back from the final step.

In chapter 4 we looked at social and economic pressures in favour of medical killing. It is not possible to isolate present discussions from deep but unspoken anxieties about these pressures. We saw a nightmarish vision of the future, where large numbers of abandoned elderly people are kept alive to suffer a pointless and degrading existence and a lonely death. In this setting a few, such as Mary Warnock, have argued that the quest for death at the end of life could be seen as a praise-worthy and altruistic response. Whether intended or not, it seems inevitable that legalization of assisted suicide would bring subtle pressures to bear on elderly people to end their lives for the welfare of others.

In chapter 5 we looked at the oldest argument for euthanasia – that from compassion. For Christian believers, the power of the argument is that it taps into a deep element of New Testament teaching. We must respond with compassion to 'the desperate cries for help of terminally ill patients'. But practical compassion should drive us not to assisted suicide, but instead to the provision of expert pain relief, psychological support and human companionship through the terminal phases of illness.

The expertise of pain specialists and the power of new pharmacological and other approaches to symptom control have never been greater. Yet, despite these remarkable advances, the pressure to legalize medical killing in the UK and elsewhere has never been so urgent. It seems that many of us have lost the belief that suffering can have any positive value at all, hence our drive to anaesthetize, to obliterate consciousness and life itself, rather than experience anything unpleasant.

At a more fundamental level, authentic Christian love says to a person, 'It's good that you exist; it's good that you are in the world.' The problem with euthanasia and assisted suicide is that in effect they say precisely the opposite: 'It's bad that you exist. It would be much better if you were not in the world.' Compassion for the agonies of suffering people with terminal illness was the primary driving force behind the development of modern palliative care, but it led not to medical killing, but to caring – skilled, costly and life-affirming.

Chapter 6 looked at the argument from autonomy. If I am genuinely the master of my fate, then surely that must mean I have the right to choose to end my life. Just like the argument from compassion, that from autonomy seems attractive to many Christian believers because it seems to chime with deep and genuine principles of the faith – here a deep concern for individual human freedom and moral responsibility. Virtually all those arguing in favour of assisting people to kill themselves add some kind of additional criteria that must be met, some additional barriers that must be circumvented. But many of these seem arbitrary, logically inconsistent and motivated more by political expediency than by principle.

The argument for autonomy rests ultimately on a profound individualism which can be traced back to the Enlightenment. But a Christian understanding of freedom starts with respect for the nature of our creation. It is only in this way that I am truly free, free to become the person that God created me to be. Even when tempted to kill out of compassion, or out of respect for individual choice, we come up against the limits of our creatureliness.

In chapter 7 we saw a Christian understanding of humanity. Our fundamental human nature is not ours to create and invent; it is given to us. We derive our meaning from outside ourselves, from God, in whose reflection we are made. Not only that, but we are created as dependent, fragile and vulnerable beings. In God's creation order we are designed to be a burden to one another, a profoundly countercultural statement in a society that prizes heroic individualism and autonomy. Here is an opportunity for the Christian community to model a different way of being fully human.

We also saw that our society, though penetrated by liberal individualism, is still deeply influenced by Christian intuitions in its commitment to suicide prevention and reduction. We are, all of us, locked together in community, bound together by duties of care, responsibility and compassion. To commit suicide is to strike at the heart of what it means to live in community, for we are designed to be dependent on one another.

As we confront the mystery of suffering, we discover that it threatens our belief that we are in ultimate control. It challenges the widespread fantasy that we can be autonomous, choosing individuals. The suffering person cannot escape the reality of his or her profound dependence on others. Here is the fundamental reason why suffering is regarded by most secular philosophers as an affront to liberal ideas of individual autonomy.

In chapter 8 we looked at medical issues raised by terminal illness. It seems that some religious people insist on receiving futile and invasive treatment at the end of life, perhaps out of fear and a desperate desire to use medical technology to hold death at bay for as long as possible. But good medical care must involve a preparedness to say 'enough is enough', and to withhold or withdraw treatment that is excessively burdensome or risky.

In place of medical killing we saw that modern palliative care provided a practical and compassionate response to the 'total pain' of the dying person. Dame Cicely Saunders and her colleagues pioneered an approach that emphasized not death, but the unexpected potential for *intense life* in the last precious days. An approach whereby 'it was possible to live a lifetime in a few weeks; that time is a matter of depth, not length; that in the right atmosphere and with pain controlled so that the patient is free to be herself, the last days can be the richest, they can be a time of reconciliation that makes the dying peaceful and the mourning bearable.'

By way of contrast, we looked at the wide-ranging and inescapable risks that assisted suicide legislation would bring: mistakes in diagnosis and prognosis, grisly failures in humane killing, risks from lethal medications in the community, abuse by relatives, progressive legislative relaxation, and psychological effects on health professionals and others.

In chapter 9 we looked in more detail at practical and medical issues concerning the care of the dying. We then examined the current legal framework for end-of-life care, the working of the Mental Capacity Act, and the potential role provided by Advance Decisions and the donation of Lasting Power of Attorney. We saw how a written statement of wishes, feelings and values could be of real assistance in aiding communication between the dying person, the healthcare team, and the family and other carers.

Dying well in the light of the future

In this brief final section I will attempt to draw together some of the profound and wonderful themes that we find in a distinctively Christian understanding of what it means to die well.

Dying need not be a totally negative experience. There is the surprising opportunity of intense and wonderful life in the last days – 'to live before you die'. As many who have gone before us have found, the end of our lives on this earth may be transformed by God's grace into an opportunity for growth and internal healing.

Of course, we must not sentimentalize what the end of life may bring. In Christian thinking, suffering is not to be sought, but there are times when it should, at least to some degree, be accepted. But the Christian faith teaches us something greater than this. In the biblical narrative, suffering and glory are inextricably linked and intertwined. In place of a simplistic utilitarian philosophy that sees suffering and pain as entirely negative and evil, the Christian faith provides a richer and more nuanced understanding. Suffering need not be all loss. In this age it cannot be abolished, but by God's grace it can be redeemed. It is a painful mystery that calls the rest of us to be a presence, to stand in community, with those who suffer.

In the biblical narrative, suffering and glory are inextricably linked and intertwined.

As we saw previously, Christian thinking affirms the importance of physical healing, while recognizing that behind our current physical experience there lies a deeper, richer, even more wonderful reality. This means that there is a time to say no to medical technology because it is time for a deeper healing, a profound transformation that medicine cannot provide.

The writer to the Hebrews tells us to 'run with persever-
ance the race marked out for us', conscious of the fact that
we are surrounded by witnesses, both our loved ones
and companions who are there with us – and an invisible
cloud of faithful witnesses who have run this race before us
(Hebrews 12:1, NIV).

Many believers have found that dying well can be an opportunity for focusing on the things that matter. A close friend of
mine who discovered that he had only a few months to live
decided that he would write a personal letter to everyone who
had been significant in his life, sharing his heart and experiences, and his faith and hope in Christ. Those last months
turned into a rich and remarkable experience that touched
hundreds of other lives. It was also obvious that my friend
was changing and growing emotionally over those last
months. While his body was deteriorating, his spirit was
growing. It was a living example of the words of Paul: 'We
do not lose heart. Though our outer self is wasting away, our
inner self is being renewed day by day' (2 Corinthians 4:16).
Dying is a paradoxical opportunity for inner growth and
renewal.

It is also an opportunity for reordering priorities, for
expressing what is really important in life. When faced with
our own imminent mortality, we learn what really matters to
us. We learn about ourselves and what is really in our hearts.
For good or ill, dying strips us of pretence and illusion, and
reveals our deepest concerns.

For some, the knowledge that life is drawing to an end
gives an opportunity for fulfilling lifelong dreams. Many have
found that it is only when they are dying that deep dreams
and longings can come to the fore. Dying gives permission
for those deep longings to be verbalized, recognized and
acknowledged.

Dying well can be an opportunity for healing from the inside. Here may be a never-to-be-repeated chance for forgiveness and starting again. For many who are facing death, it is relational pain, the agony of broken and twisted relationships, that is often the deepest suffering. But as we've seen, here is an opportunity for restoration and reconciliation, if only it can be grasped. In those last days and weeks the relational pain of the dying person can often be healed in a remarkable and life-transforming manner.

Dying well is an opportunity for saying sorry and thank you to those who matter to us. It is also an opportunity for encouraging those who remain. To previous generations the last words of the dying believer were seen as profoundly important and significant, to be treasured, reflected on and heeded. Sadly, with the medicalized nature of death, this tradition has been lost – but perhaps it can be recovered in some form within the Christian community? The formal written statement of wishes and values that was referred to in the previous chapter could also become a way of encouraging and challenging those who remain.

Finally, dying well is an opportunity for letting go, for relinquishing tasks that will never be fulfilled, for accepting with grace that the secular myth of a life as a self-directed and controlling individual must be abandoned. It is a time for reminding oneself that Christ has triumphed over death, that at the cross he drained death of its terrible power and curse, and that forgiveness for past sin and guilt is offered freely. It is a time for remembering that perfect love casts out fear. It is a time for recognizing the element of passivity which goes with the true understanding of suffering, and for surrendering ourselves into the everlasting arms that lie beneath, in the sure and certain hope of waking again to see the face of the One who has loved us with an eternal love:

As for me, I shall behold your face in righteousness;
  when I awake, I shall be satisfied with your likeness.
(Psalm 17:15)

I know that my Redeemer lives,
  and at the last he will stand upon the earth.
And after my skin has been thus destroyed,
  yet in my flesh I shall see God,
whom I shall see for myself,
  and my eyes shall behold, and not another.
  My heart faints within me!
(Job 19:25–27)

When he appears we shall be like him, because we shall see
him as he is.
(1 John 3:2)

We are still called to walk the valley of the shadow of death, but we do so in the knowledge that God himself is with us. He too, in the person of Jesus, has experienced the reality of death, and he has defeated it. Death has lost its sting. It is very significant that in the New Testament Scriptures believers are not described as 'dying'; instead they 'fall asleep'. The terrors of death have been destroyed for ever in the resurrection life of Christ.

I will close with the words of John Donne:

Death, be not proud, though some have called thee
Mighty and dreadful, for thou art not so;
For those whom thou think'st thou dost overthrow
Die not, poor Death, nor yet canst thou kill me . . .
One short sleep past, we wake eternally
And death shall be no more; Death, thou shalt die.

Appendix 1

Example Statement of Wishes and Values for a Christian believer

I recognize that my current illness is unlikely to be cured and that it is likely to lead to my death. As a Christian believer, this is not something that I fear. I look forward to going to be with Jesus Christ, who has promised me eternal life through his death and resurrection. I know he will be with me to comfort and support me whatever the future holds.

I am grateful for the medical and nursing care I am receiving at this time of need. I would like to be actively involved in all decisions both about my care and about those individuals and agencies that are involved in my care.

Where it is possible, I wish to be consulted about all decisions relevant to my care and to participate in those decisions. However, if I should ever lose the ability to participate actively in decision-making, I would like the following principles to be respected when decisions need to be made:

I would like to be kept as free from pain and other distressing symptoms as possible.

I would like to retain the ability to communicate with family and friends, if at all possible, and not to be given treatment intended to reduce my level of consciousness unnecessarily.

I would never want to receive any intervention or treatment designed to end my life, regardless of how my level of suffering may be perceived by others.

(*Optional sentence*) In the case of an acute deterioration in my condition, I would like to receive active medical treatment that has a reasonable chance of prolonging my life and preserving function.

(*Optional sentence*) I would wish to receive clinically assisted nutrition and/or hydration if these have a reasonable chance of prolonging my life or of alleviating my symptoms and if they are not causing me evident distress.

If my condition is deteriorating irretrievably, and in the view of the medical and nursing teams looking after me, there is no realistic hope of recovery, I would accept and welcome palliative treatment instead of further attempts at active medical management.

I would not want to cling on to life in this world because I have a living hope of life after death and of a wonderful future with my Lord Jesus Christ.

My life as part of a local church community is very important to me. I would not wish my church friends to be denied access from visiting me. In particular, I value ongoing spiritual and personal support from my church leaders and from other friends, including the following named individuals:

....

If I am ever unable to participate in decisions about my care, I wish the following named individuals to be actively involved in the decision-making process:

....

Signed ....

Witnessed ....

Date ....

(adapted from *Facing Serious Illness: Guidance for Christians towards the End of Life*, Christian Medical Fellowship, 2015)

This appendix quotes from the 2011 position paper of the Royal Dutch Medical Association (KNMG) entitled 'The Role of the Physician in the Voluntary Termination of Life'.

I have quoted it in some detail because it seems highly significant in describing the pressures and conflicts that many doctors in the Netherlands now experience because of the availability of legalized euthanasia.

Society has high expectations. This public pressure is perceived as both burdensome and risky by physicians, who cite society's stigmatisation of the aged and people with dementia. Dementia, for example, is portrayed as one of society's urgent problems, partly in view of the estimated numbers of people expected to be affected by this syndrome in decades to come, and based on the premise that dementia necessarily leads to a poor quality of life and an undignified death.

The KNMG wishes to emphasise that euthanasia is an exceptional medical procedure that inherently entails a dilemma for the physician requested to perform it and will never become 'standard'.

There will continue to be plenty of physicians who are either unwilling or morally indisposed to be able and willing to make full use of the statutory freedom, to which society is laying an increasingly vocal claim as integral to its right to self-determination. It is important to recognise that physicians are insufficiently aware of the fact that patients in early (or late) stages of dementia or chronic psychiatric illness have equal recourse to the Termination of Life on Request and Assisted Suicide (Review Procedures) Act.

Yet we also know that any assessment of the considerations prompting such a request, and of whether the suffering is indeed unbearable and lasting, is generally much more complicated in this category of patients than among those who are suffering due to somatic problems and ailments. It is in part for this reason, and the threat of criminal proceedings, that physicians act with extreme caution and restraint in such situations. The KNMG feels such restraint is justified.

The KNMG's position paper also demonstrates that an accumulation of geriatric afflictions, including loss of function, that result in progressive deterioration may also qualify as unbearable and lasting suffering within the meaning of the Termination of Life on Request and Assisted Suicide (Review Procedures) Act. However, there must always be a medical basis in such cases, meaning that the patient must have a condition that is defined as a disease or combination of diseases/ailments. Of course, this is precisely the physician's domain of expertise. In the KNMG's view, physicians can benefit greatly from consulting colleagues and/or other professionals in order to take stock of all alternatives. A physician's first duty, after all, is that of care.

Equally, a physician has a duty of care when a patient with a strong wish to die has no recourse to the Termination of Life on Request and Assisted Suicide (Review Procedures) Act or is refused by his physician and chooses to deny food and drink on his own initiative. In that case, the physician not only should inform the patient as thoroughly as possible about the pros and cons, but also ultimately bears a duty of care to prepare and supervise the patient and to implement palliative care or, where medically indicated, palliative sedation.

Patients, too, often have difficulty telling a physician they have an authentic wish to die. Physicians, for their part, are under an obligation to take such requests seriously. This also means that if a physician cannot or does not wish to honour a patient's request for euthanasia or assisted suicide, he must give the patient a timely and clear explanation of why, and furthermore must then refer or transfer the patient to another physician in good time. Vague promises, failure to transfer patients during absences, causing delays or indicating at a late stage or too late that the physician has reconsidered his decision to perform the euthanasia, all demonstrate a lack of professionalism. The KNMG therefore calls on all physicians to act as they would wish themselves or their loved ones to be treated.

A paper published in the academic journal *Bioethics* in 2012 illustrates the way in which ethical arguments are being put forward in favour of euthanasia combined with organ donation:

> There are not enough solid organs available to meet the needs of patients with organ failure. Thousands of patients every year die on the waiting lists for transplantation. Yet there is one currently available, underutilized, potential source of organs. Many patients die in intensive care following withdrawal of life-sustaining treatment whose organs could be used to save the lives of others. At present the majority of these organs go to waste . . .
>
> An alternative would be to anaesthetize the patient and remove organs, including the heart and lungs. Brain death would follow removal of the heart (call this Organ Donation Euthanasia) . . . The process of death would be less likely to be associated with suffering for the patient than death following withdrawal of life-sustaining treatment (which is not usually accompanied by full anaesthetic doses of drugs). If there were a careful and appropriate process for selection, no patient would die who would not otherwise have died. Organs would be more likely to be viable, since they would not have sustained a period of reduced circulation prior to retrieval. More organs would be available (for example the heart and lungs, which are currently rarely available in the setting of donation following circulatory death). Patients and families could be reassured that their organs would be able to help other individuals as long as there were recipients available, and there were no contraindications to transplantation.

Report of the Liverpool Care Pathway Review Panel

The review panel provided a report entitled 'More Care, Less Pathway'. The panel concluded that the LCP was not being applied properly in many cases, and that generic protocols were the wrong approach. The panel recommended the development of a series of guides and alerts reflecting the common principles of good palliative care, supplemented by technical guidance specific to certain disease groups. It was recommended that use of the LCP should be replaced by an end-of-life care plan for each patient, together with good-practice guidance for the patient's specific condition.

The report highlighted that there was often a lack of availability of staff to care for the dying, in terms of both the numbers and the level of competence, together with fragmentation of care teams between hospitals, community and hospices, and a lack of continuity of care. The panel recommended that

> every patient diagnosed as dying should have a clearly
> identified senior responsible clinician accountable for their
> care during any 'out of hours' period. Unless it is unavoidable,
> urgent, and is clearly in the patient's best interests, the decision
> to withdraw or not to start a life-prolonging treatment should
> be taken in the cool light of day by the senior responsible
> clinician in consultation with the healthcare team.

The review panel highlighted the importance of good communication between healthcare staff, relatives and patients:

Unless there has been good communication between staff and relatives or carers, unnecessary misunderstandings and distress can arise. Care of the dying requires not only substantial technical knowledge and clinical skill, but above all it needs excellent communication skills. Adequate training and continued support is the key to getting this aspect of care right . . .

The report also highlighted the importance of the need for open and honest discussion about death and dying within the population as a whole:

No matter how much effort is put into training clinicians in good communication skills, unless everyone in society – members of the public, the press, clinicians, public figures – is prepared to talk openly and honestly about dying, death and bereavement, accepting these as a normal part of life, the quality of care and the range of services for the dying, their relatives and carers will remain inconsistent.

Provision of fluids and assisted nutrition

An area of particular concern and controversy has been the provision of fluids and assisted nutrition to dying patients. There have been many concerns that dying patients were deliberately deprived of fluids and nutrition by clinical staff.

During the phase when the person is 'actively dying', a phase that usually lasts hours or a few days at most, it is common for there to be a reduced desire to eat and drink. A dying person may decide that he or she does not wish to eat. With regard to fluids, many people also have a reduced desire to drink. However, if fluids are withheld over many days, then death from dehydration will be inevitable, and the lack of hydration will have accelerated the dying process. Inadequate hydration is a real vulnerability for old and frail people.

Hence, it has become accepted that the default course of action in caring for patients in the terminal phase should be that patients are offered oral hydration and nutrition unless there is a strong clinical reason not to do so (such as where it is impossible for the person to absorb fluids orally).

Giving fluids by the intravenous, subcutaneous or naso-gastric route (often called 'clinically assisted hydration') may not be helpful in the dying patient. Fluid overload easily occurs, leading to tissue swelling or oedema, and the lungs may fill with fluid, causing breathing difficulties. A systematic review of the scientific literature showed no evidence of clear benefit of clinically assisted hydration in patients who were receiving palliative care. Fluid administration did not appear to lengthen life or improve the patient's well-being at the end of life.

Hence, there is no clear moral or legal imperative to provide clinically assisted hydration in dying patients. What is important is that the benefits and risks of this form of hydration must be balanced, and the course of action should be that which is genuinely in the person's best interests. Where possible, this discussion should be had with the person in question, so that his or her own wishes and concerns can be expressed. If it does seem likely that clinically assisted hydration will increase the comfort of the dying person, it may be more appropriate to give subcutaneous fluids rather than an intravenous infusion, since the subcutaneous route is easier to manage.

Terminal sedation

This is a complex and controversial subject, and I can deal with it only briefly here. As was referred to in chapter 2, there has been a notable trend in the Netherlands for the use of what is called 'palliative sedation' in patients at the end of life. In an official report the Royal Dutch Medical Association (KNMG) defined palliative sedation as the deliberate lowering of a patient's level of consciousness in the last stages of life. It may involve continuous sedation until the moment of death, or temporary or intermittent sedation. This practice usually involves continuous intravenous infusions of sedatives, but no hydration or nutrition. It may be given for periods of up to one to two weeks, after which death is inevitable.

The KNMG report stated that continuous sedation to death was appropriate where pain was unbearable and hopeless. The report also stated that

in addition to pain, 'existential suffering' may be among the refractory symptoms that go to make up unbearable suffering. Such suffering cannot be alleviated, for instance by communication or spiritual support. These patients are often extremely ill and weak, close to death, and have a range of physical complaints, some of them often severe. Some do not want to experience their final days consciously and may request continuous sedation. The feeling that one's existence is empty or meaningless, which is what we mean by existential suffering, may cause unbearable suffering . . . The focus here is on the meaninglessness of existence when death is expected within one or two weeks.

In the Netherlands this practice is regarded as part of palliative care, and it is not regarded as a form of euthanasia. Hence, it does not require official reporting. As discussed in chapter 2, it has been estimated that it accounted for about 8% of deaths in 2005, rising to about 12% in 2010.

In the UK, and most other countries, to induce prolonged unconsciousness by sedation without providing hydration would be regarded as hastening death, unless the patient was in the terminal phase and considered as 'actively dying'. In other words, terminal sedation would only be appropriate where patients were likely to die within a few hours or at most one or two days. If the patient had not died of natural causes within one or two days, it would be normal practice to withdraw sedation and allow the patient to wake up.

With the highest quality of palliative care, most patients approaching death are settled and comfortable. However, there is a minority who remain restless, anxious and deeply distressed despite appropriate care. Experienced palliative care staff recognize that this is often because of underlying psychological, relational or spiritual issues – 'existential suffering' in the language of the KNMG. As we saw earlier, they would endeavour to identify and address 'the question behind the question'.

If the patient remains very distressed despite all measures to help, it may be appropriate to render them unconscious with sedative drugs for a period of approximately twenty-four or so hours, followed by gradual removal of sedation. Experience has shown that a period of medicated sleep may be enough to cause the acute distress to be ameliorated, allowing engagement with carers and family. This form of temporary sedation is part of the therapeutic options of modern palliative care, but it is a long way from the practice of terminal sedation described in the KNMG report.

Notes and references

1. Recent cases and media debates

Martin Amis's comments were widely reported in the UK press
on 24 January 2010. See http://www.martinamisweb.com/
commentary_files/euthanasiabooths_I.pdf.

Edward and Joan Downes's story was reported in the *London
Evening Standard* on 14 July 2009: http://www.standard.co.uk/
news/bbc-conductor-sir-edward-downes-and-wife-commit-
suicide-6718179.html.

The decision of the Director of Public Prosecution was reported
on the Crown Prosecution Service website on 19 March 2010:
http://www.cps.gov.uk/news/latest_news/113_10/.

For Daniel James's story, see *The Independent* website on
18 October 2008: http://www.independent.co.uk/news/uk/
home-news/at-23-daniel-chose-to-end-his-second-class-
life-965447.html.

Baroness Mary Warnock's comments can be found on the
Guardian website: http://www.theguardian.com/
commentisfree/2008/oct/19/euthanasia-daniel-james-health-law.

Tony Nicklinson's story was widely reported on 12 March 2012. See http://www.dailymail.co.uk/news/article-2113782/Tony-Nicklinsons-right-die-victory-Ive-got-dignity-left-I-want-die.html.

The High Court judgment was announced on 16 August 2012. See http://www.telegraph.co.uk/news/uknews/law-and-order/9480227/Tony-Nicklinson-breaks-down-as-High-Court-rejects-his-right-to-die-plea.html.

Tony Nicklinson's death was reported on 22 August 2012. See http://www.theguardian.com/uk/2012/aug/22/tony-nicklinson-right-to-die-case.

The obituary of Nan Maitland can be found on the Homeshare website: http://homeshare.org/wp-content/uploads/2012/04/Nan_Maitland_obit_March_2011.pdf.

The comments of Ludwig Minelli were reported on 20 September 2006: http://www.dailymail.co.uk/news/article-406174/Clinically-depressed-allowed-assisted-suicide.html.

2. History of euthanasia and international scene

For the history of euthanasia in the UK, see Nick Kemp, *'Merciful Release': The History of the British Euthanasia Movement* (Manchester University Press, 2002).

For euthanasia practices in Nazi Germany, see R. Proctor, *Racial Hygiene: Medicine under the Nazis* (Harvard University Press, 1988). See also J. Wyatt, *Matters of Life and Death*, 2nd edn (Inter-Varsity Press, 2009), ch. 9.

The film *Ich Klage An* is available from a number of internet sources. See for example https://www.youtube.com/watch?v=sfMjUCSx4JE.

Detailed information about Aktion T4 is available from many internet sources. See for example http://en.wikipedia.org/wiki/Action_T4.

Leo Alexander's paper was published in *New England Journal of Medicine* (1949), 241: 39–47.

Details about the legal basis of euthanasia in the Netherlands are derived from P. Lewis, *Assisted Dying and Legal Change* (Oxford University Press, 2007). See this volume for further information.

Information about NVVE can be obtained from their website: https://www.nvve.nl/about-nvve.

For the Remmelink report, see P. J. van der Maas et al., *Lancet* (1991), 338: 669–674. In the report, reasons given by doctors for euthanasia included absence of any prospect of improvement, needless prolongation of life, the relatives' inability to cope, and low quality of life. Pain and suffering were mentioned in only 30% of cases. When the reasons that patients themselves gave for requesting euthanasia were analysed, 57% said it was 'loss of dignity', 46% 'not dying in a dignified way', 46% mentioned 'pain', 33% 'dependence' and 23% 'tiredness of life'.

Since then there have been two other major nationwide surveys of euthanasia in the Netherlands: P. J. van der Maas et al., *New England Journal of Medicine* (1996), 335: 1699–1705; A. van der Heide et al., *New England Journal of Medicine* (2007), 356: 1957–1965.

For detailed information about palliative sedation in the Netherlands, see R. Janssens et al., 'Palliative Sedation: Not Just Normal Medical Practice. Ethical Reflections on the Royal Dutch Medical Association's Guideline on Palliative Sedation', *Journal of Medical Ethics* doi:10.1136/medethics-2011-100353.

For information about the Chabot case, see J. Griffiths, *Modern Law Review* (1995), 52: 2 March: http://www.jstor.org/discover/10.2307/1096356?uid=3738032&uid=2&uid=4&sid=21106443689361.

The interview with Dr Paulan Stärcke is available from the NVVE website: https://www.nvve.nl/files/2013/8753/1322/Relevant_2013-2.pdf.

The rise in euthanasia in psychiatric patients was reported in the *New York Times* on 11 February 2014: http://www.nltimes.nl/2014/02/11/patients-psychiatric-disorder-often-euthanised/.

The reference for the Groningen Protocol is E. Verhagen and P. Sauer, *New England Journal of Medicine* (2005), 352: 959–962. The survey of end-of-life decisions in neonates and infants is published as: A. van der Heide et al., *Lancet* (1997), 350: 251–255.

The KNMG position paper can be downloaded from the KNMG website: http://knmg.artsennet.nl/Publicaties/KNMGpublicatie/100696/Position-paper-The-role-of-the-physician-in-the-voluntary-termination-of-life-2011.htm.

Information about the NVVE End of Life clinic was published in the *Guardian* newspaper on 1 March 2012: http://www.theguardian.com/world/2012/mar/01/dutch-mobile-euthanasia-units. Further information is available from the NVVE website and other internet sources such as http://www.worldrtd.net/sites/default/files/newsfiles/Summaries%202013-1%20NVVE.pdf.

Information about the film by Dr Chabot and the film festival is available from the Radio Netherlands website: https://www.rnw.org/archive/self-help-film-gives-instructions-euthanasia.

Information about the Oregon Death with Dignity Act is available from many sources, including annual reports provided by the Oregon Public Health Division: https://public.health.oregon.gov/ProviderPartnerResources/EvaluationResearch/DeathwithDignityAct/Documents/year17.pdf.

For the comments of the Oregon doctor, see evidence to the 2004 Select Committee on Assisted Dying Bill: http://www.publications.parliament.uk/pa/ld200405/ldselect/ldasdy/86/4120922.htm.

For the comments of the Dutch euthanasia specialists, see evidence to the 2004 Select Committee on Assisted Dying Bill: http://www.publications.parliament.uk/pa/ld200405/ldselect/ldasdy/86/4121010.htm.

The February 2015 Judgment of the Canada Supreme Court is available at https://scc-csc.lexum.com/scc-csc/scc-csc/en/item/14637/index.do.

The 2002 Belgium Euthanasia Act is available at http://www.ethical-perspectives.be/viewpic.php?TABLE=EP&ID=59.

The paper on euthanasia in psychiatric patients is: K. Naudts et al., 'Euthanasia: The Role of the Psychiatrist', *British Journal of Psychiatry* (2006), 188: 405–409. It can be downloaded at http://bjp.rcpsych.org/content/bjprcpsych/188/5/405.full.pdf.

A news report about euthanasia in children in Belgium is available at http://www.reuters.com/article/2013/11/26/us-belgium-euthanasia-idUSBRE9AP13T20131126.

The Dignitas clinic website is available at http://www.dignitas.ch/index.php?option=com%20_content&view=article&id=23&lang=en.

The comments of Ludwig Minelli were reported on 20 September 2006: http://www.dailymail.co.uk/news/article-406174/Clinically-depressed-allowed-assisted-suicide.html.

Up-to-date information about euthanasia developments in the Netherlands, Oregon, Belgium and elsewhere is available from the Care Not Killing website: www.carenotkilling.org.uk/.

3. United Kingdom experience

More details about the history of euthanasia in the UK are available in Nick Kemp, *'Merciful Release': The History of the British Euthanasia Movement* (Manchester University Press, 2002).

Information about the history of the publication of self-help material is at http://www.finalexit.org/how_to_books_on_self-deliverance_and_euthanasia.html.

A summary of the conclusions of the 1994 Select Committee on Medical Ethics is available in Hansard for 9 May 1994:

http://hansard.millbanksystems.com/lords/1994/may/09/
medical-ethics-select-committee-report.

Lord Joffe's 2006 Assisted Dying for the Terminally Ill Bill is
available at http://www.publications.parliament.uk/pa/
ld200506/ldbills/036/06036.i.html.

Information about the name change of the Voluntary Euthanasia
Society is available from the Dignity in Dying website: http://
www.dignityindying.org.uk/press-release/voluntary-euthanasia-
society-changes-name-after-70-years-to-become-dignity-in-dying-
23-jan/.

The report of the Falconer Commission on Assisted Dying can be
downloaded from the Demos website: http://www.demos.co.uk/
publications/thecommissiononassisteddying.

The 2014 Assisted Dying Bill is available from the UK Parliament
website: http://services.parliament.uk/bills/2014-15/
assisteddying.html, and the 2015 Assisted Dying Bill at http://
services.parliament.uk/bills/2015-16/assisteddyingno2.html.

The quotation about the Members of Parliament being
'ridiculously out of touch with the British public' is taken from
a press release from Dignity in Dying released immediately after
the debate: http://www.dignityindying.org.uk/press-release/
parliament-ignores-public-votes-assisted-dying-bill/.

Up-to-date information about proposed legalization of assisted
suicide in England and Scotland is available from the Care Not
Killing website: www.carenotkilling.org.uk/.

4. Underlying forces

The quotation from Prof. Nigel Biggar is taken from an article in
Standpoint magazine: http://standpointmag.co.uk/text-march-10-
the-road-to-death-on-demand-nigel-biggar-assisted-suicide?page=0
%2C0%2C0%2C0%2C0%2C0%2C0%2C0%2C0%2C0%2C0%2C3.

The precise numbers and projections are inevitably constantly changing. Perhaps the most accurate and regularly updated statistics on the elderly population in the UK are published by Age UK: http://www.ageuk.org.uk/Documents/EN-GB/Factsheets/Later_Life_UK_factsheet.pdf?dtrk=true.

Statistics on the global population of the elderly are available from a 2013 United Nations Report: http://www.un.org/en/development/desa/population/publications/pdf/ageing/WorldPopulationAgeing2013.pdf and from the World Health Organisation: http://www.who.int/ageing/en/.

Information about isolation and contacts of elderly people is available in the 2012 report of the Women's Royal Voluntary Service (WRVS), 'Loneliness amongst Older People and the Impact of Family Connections': http://www.royalvoluntaryservice.org.uk/Uploads/Documents/How_we_help/loneliness-amongst-older-people-and-the-impact-of-family-connections.pdf.

International statistics on elderly people is available in the Overseas Development Institute (ODI) report, 'Old Age, Disability and Mental Health': http://www.managingforimpact.org/sites/default/files/resource/odi_old_age_note.pdf.

Information about the health consequences of loneliness are in the WRVS report: http://www.royalvoluntaryservice.org.uk/Uploads/Documents/How_we_help/loneliness-amongst-older-people-and-the-impact-of-family-connections.pdf.

Information and statistics about Alzheimer's disease are available from the Alzheimer's Society website: http://www.alzheimers.org.uk/site/scripts/documents_info.php?documentID=341.

The tragic story of John and Meryl Parry was published on the BBC News website on 3 July 2015: http://www.bbc.co.uk/news/uk-england-cumbria-33376317.

Information about economic consequences is available from the UK Parliament website: http://www.parliament.uk/business/publications/research/key-issues-for-the-new-parliament/value-for-money-in-public-services/the-ageing-population/.

Mary Warnock's book, *Easeful Death*, was published in 2008 by Oxford University Press.

The interview with Baroness Mary Warnock was reported on 18 September 2008: http://www.telegraph.co.uk/news/uknews/2983652/Baroness-Warnock-Dementia-sufferers-may-have-a-duty-to-die.html.

The information on organ transplantation after euthanasia in Belgium is taken from D. Ysebaert et al., 'Organ Procurement after Euthanasia: Belgian Experience', *Transplant Proceedings* (2009), 41: 585–586.

Further information about organ donation following euthanasia in Belgium is available at http://deredactie.be/cm/vrtnieuws/binnenland/1.1443262. See also Dominic Wilkinson and Julian Savulescu, 'Should We Allow Organ Donation Euthanasia?', *Bioethics* (2012), 26: 32–48, available at http://www.ncbi.nlm.nih.gov/pmc/articles/PMC3267048/pdf/bioe0026-0032.pdf.

Information about human overpopulation and carrying capacity is available in the Wikipedia article: http://en.wikipedia.org/wiki/Human_overpopulation.

5. The argument from compassion

The words of Jasper Conran were taken from http://www.dignityindying.org.uk/patron/jasper-conran/.

The words of Lord Joffe were taken from http://www.dignityindying.org.uk/patron/lord-joel-joffe-cbe/.

Rev. Paul Badham's words can be found on the Dignity in Dying website: http://www.dignityindying.org.uk/blog/christian-case-assisted-dying/.

The full text of the debate in the House of Lords on 18 July 2014 is available from the UK Parliament website: http://www.publications.parliament.uk/pa/ld201415/ldhansrd/text/140718-0001.htm#14071854000545.

A helpful summary of contributions to the House of Lords debate is available on the Law and Religion UK website: http://www.lawandreligionuk.com/2014/07/19/lord-falconers-assisted-dying-bill-second-reading/.

The report of the Falconer Commission on Assisted Dying can be downloaded from the Demos website: http://www.demos.co.uk/publications/thecommissiononassisteddying.

The tragic story of Nathan Verhelst was reported in various newspapers on 1 October 2013. See http://www.telegraph.co.uk/news/worldnews/europe/belgium/10346616/Belgian-killed-by-euthanasia-after-a-botched-sex-change-operation.html.

The words of Karl Brandt are quoted in J. A. Vermaat, '"Euthanasia" in the Third Reich: Lessons for Today?' *Ethics and Medicine* (2002), vol. 18:1.

For more on the profound thought of Josef Pieper, see his book, *Faith, Hope, Love* (Ignatius Press, 1997).

For further discussion about the meaning and role of compassion in suicide and euthanasia, see Nigel Biggar, *Aiming to Kill: The Ethics of Suicide and Euthanasia* (Pilgrim, 2004).

6. The argument from autonomy

The words of Terry Pratchett are taken from the Dignity in Dying website: http://www.dignityindying.org.uk/about-us/patrons/.

The words of A. C. Grayling are taken from the Dignity in Dying website: http://www.dignityindying.org.uk/about-us/patrons/.

The quotation from John Harris is from J. Harris, 'Consent and End of Life Decisions', *Journal of Medical Ethics* (2003), 29: 10–15.

The 'Invictus' poem can be found on the Poetry Foundation website: http://www.poetryfoundation.org/poem/182194.

The text of John Stuart Mill's book, *On Liberty*, can be found on the Project Gutenberg website: https://www.gutenberg.org/files/34901/34901-h/34901-h.htm.

Ronald Dworkin's words are from his book, *Life's Dominion* (HarperCollins, 1995).

The words of Desmond Tutu are from the *Guardian* newspaper on 12 July 2014: http://www.theguardian.com/commentisfree/2014/jul/12/desmond-tutu-in-favour-of-assisted-dying.

The case of Miss B is *Re B (Adult: Refusal of Medical Treatment)* EWHC (2002) 2 All England Reports 449.

The report of the Falconer Commission on Assisted Dying can be downloaded from the Demos website: http://www.demos.co.uk/publications/thecommissiononassisteddying.

The paper on assisted suicide in patients with depression is U. Schuklenk and S. van de Vathorst, 'Treatment-Resistant Major Depressive Disorder and Assisted Dying', *Journal of Medical Ethics* (2015); published online 2 May 2015.

The reasons for assisted suicide in Oregon are reported annually by the Oregon Public Health Division: https://public.health.oregon.gov/ProviderPartnerResources/EvaluationResearch/DeathwithDignityAct/Documents/year17.pdf.

7. Christian responses and perspectives

The quotation from Gilbert Meilaender is in his book *Bioethics: A Primer for Christians* (Eerdmans, 2005).

Cicero's words are from *De finibus bonorum et malorum*, trans. H. Rackham (W. Heinemann, 1914), pp. 60–61.

The quotations from doctors who practised euthanasia are from a paper by Kenneth Stevens, Jr, entitled 'Emotional and Psychological Effects of Physician-Assisted Suicide and Euthanasia on Participating Physicians', *Issues in Law and Medicine* (2006), 21: 187, available at http://www.pccef.org/articles/art44.htm.

John Donne's words are taken from 'Devotions upon Emergent Occasions', *Meditations* XVII, 1624. It is available at the Literature Network website: http://www.online-literature.com/donne/409/.

The quotations from Stanley Hauerwas are from his book *Suffering Presence* (University of Notre Dame Press, 1986), p. 48.

8. Medical issues in the care of the dying person

The study of dying people in the USA is A. C. Phelps et al., 'Religious Coping and Use of Intensive Life-Prolonging Care Near Death in Patients with Advanced Cancer', *JAMA* (2009), 301: 1140–1147. It can be downloaded at http://jama.jamanetwork.com/article.aspx?articleid=183578.

A helpful review of the evidence that opiates in palliative care rarely hasten death is S. Anderson, 'The Double Effect of Pain Medication: Separating Myth from Reality', *Journal of Palliative Medicine* (1998), 1: 315–328. It is available at http://hospicecare.com/resources/ethical-issues/essays-and-articles-on-ethics-in-palliative-care/the-double-effect-of-pain-medication-separating-myth-from-reality/.

The words of Margaret Mead are quoted by N. Cameron, *The New Medicine* (Hodder & Stoughton, 1991), p. 9.

Much of the material about Cicely Saunders is taken from Shirley du Boulay's book, *Cicely Saunders: The Founder of the Modern Hospice Movement*, updated, with additional chapters by Marianne Rankin (SPCK, 2007).

Further material about her life and work is available from the Cicely Saunders International website: http://cicelysaundersinternational.org/dame-cicely-saunders/.

The words of Dr Robert Twycross are from his book, *Introducing Palliative Care* (Radcliffe Medical Press, 2003).

An obituary of Abdul Abdelbaset al-Megrahi can be found at http://www.bbc.co.uk/news/uk-scotland-12174643.

The study of the complications of euthanasia and assisted suicide is J. H. Groenewoud et al., 'Clinical Problems with the Performance of Euthanasia and Physician-Assisted Suicide in the Netherlands', *New England Journal of Medicine* (2000), 342: 551–556. It can be downloaded at http://www.nejm.org/doi/pdf/10.1056/NEJM200002243420805.

The quotation from the Dutch doctor is from D. C. Thomasma (ed.), *Asking to Die: Inside the Dutch Debate about Euthanasia* (Klewer Academic, 2000).

The report of the Falconer Commission on Assisted Dying can be downloaded from the Demos website: http://www.demos.co.uk/publications/thecommissiononassisteddying.

9. Palliative care and legal frameworks

Some of the material, including the words of Baroness Illora Finlay, is taken from George Pitcher, *A Time to Live* (Monarch, 2010).

Other material in this chapter is taken from *Facing Serious Illness: Guidance for Christians towards the End of Life* (Christian Medical Fellowship, 2015).

A detailed and thoughtful discussion of the philosophy of palliative care is available in Fiona Randall and Robin Downie, *The Philosophy of Palliative Care: Critique and Reconstruction* (Oxford University Press, 2006).

The Palliative Care Funding Review, *Funding the Right Care and Support for Everyone*, is available at https://www.gov.uk/government/uploads/system/uploads/attachment_data/file/215107/dh_133105.pdf.

Information about the funding of independent hospices in the UK is available from Hospice UK: www.hospiceuk.org.

The report of the Independent Review of the Liverpool Care Pathway is available at https://www.gov.uk/government/uploads/system/uploads/attachment_data/file/212450/Liverpool_Care_Pathway.pdf.

Detailed information about the UK Mental Capacity Act 2005 is available at http://www.legislation.gov.uk/ukpga/2005/9/contents and from the Code of Practice 2013 at https://www.gov.uk/government/uploads/system/uploads/attachment_data/file/224660/Mental_Capacity_Act_code_of_practice.pdf.

Information and guidance about Lasting Power of Attorney is available from the UK government website at https://www.gov.uk/power-of-attorney/overview.

Information and guidance about Advance Decisions is available from an official NHS website at http://www.adrt.nhs.uk.

10. Dying well and dying faithfully

The poem by John Donne is 'Death, Be Not Proud', from *Holy Sonnets*, no. 10, published in 1633, and can be found on the Poetry Foundation website: http://www.poetryfoundation.org/poem/173363.

Appendix notes

The KNMG position paper, 'The Role of the Physician in the Voluntary Termination of Life', can be downloaded at http://knmg.artsennet.nl/Publicaties/KNMGpublicatie/100696/Position-paper-The-role-of-the-physician-in-the-voluntary-termination-of-life-2011.htm.

The paper on organ donation after euthanasia is Dominic Wilkinson and Julian Savulescu, 'Should We Allow Organ Donation Euthanasia?', *Bioethics* (2012), 26: 32–48. It can be downloaded at http://www.ncbi.nlm.nih.gov/pmc/articles/PMC3267048/pdf/bioe0026-0032.pdf.

The report of the Independent Review of the Liverpool Care Pathway is available at https://www.gov.uk/government/uploads/system/uploads/attachment_data/file/212450/Liverpool_Care_Pathway.pdf.

Official guidance for UK doctors on clinically assisted nutrition and hydration at the end of life is available from the General Medical Council website: http://www.gmc-uk.org/guidance/ethical_guidance/end_of_life_clinically_assisted_nutrition_and_hydration.asp.

Systematic review, P. Good et al., 'Medically Assisted Hydration for Adult Palliative Care Patients' (2010), Cochrane Library, is available at http://scholar.google.co.uk/scholar_url?url=http://www.researchgate.net/profile/Phillip_Good/publication/5426799_Medically_assisted_hydration_for_palliative_care_patients/links/02e7e5278504605732000000.pdf&hl=en&sa=X&scisig=AAGBfmoMnbxnz9OCn6wL99sAetRl4BJaiw&nossl=1&oi=scholarr&ei=eoFbVciiJsiR7AaZhIGwBg&ved=0CCAQgAMoADAA.

The Royal Dutch Medical Association guideline on palliative sedation is available at http://palliativedrugs.com/download/091110_KNMG_Guideline_for_Palliative_sedation_2009__2_[1].pdf.

For detailed information about palliative sedation in the Netherlands, see R. Janssens et al., 'Palliative Sedation: Not Just Normal Medical Practice. Ethical Reflections on the Royal Dutch Medical Association's Guideline on Palliative Sedation', *Journal of Medical Ethics* doi:10.1136/medethics-2011-100353.

Glossary of medical and technical terms

Advance Decision. A legally binding document, sometimes referred to as a 'living will', that is used to refuse consent to specific treatments, such as life-sustaining treatments, in the future. See further discussion in chapter 9.

Alzheimer's disease. The most common form of dementia (see below for definition), leading to a progressive decline in mental functioning due to gradual death of brain cells. The cause is still unknown.

Anorexia nervosa. A serious mental health condition and eating disorder, leading to compulsive weight restriction.

Assisted dying. A recently employed euphemism for assisted suicide (see below), used only in the UK.

Assisted suicide (also called physician-assisted suicide or medically assisted suicide). The prescription and supply of lethal drugs by a doctor to a patient, at their request, in order to ensure that they kill themselves without complications. See chapter 3 for more information.

Autonomy. The philosophical principle of self-rule or self-governance. An autonomous choice is one that, in theory, an individual makes of his or her own free will, without being coerced or manipulated.

Barbiturate. A sedative drug that is potentially lethal in overdose. It is no longer used in medical practice for sedation because of the risks of overdose.

Chloroform. A powerful anaesthetic drug discovered in the nineteenth century that is lethal in overdose.

Clinically assisted nutrition and hydration. The provision of liquid food or fluids by a tube or intravenous line in a patient who is unable to take sufficient food or fluids by mouth.

Dementia. A general term for any form of medical condition leading to a progressive decline in mental functioning. There are many different kinds of dementia, but Alzheimer's disease is the most common.

Eugenics. A scientific movement starting in the nineteenth century intended to improve the genetic features of human populations through selective breeding of 'genetically fit' individuals and forced sterilization of those who were deemed 'genetically unfit'.

Euthanasia (also called mercy killing). The intentional medical killing, by act or omission, of an individual whose life is thought to be not worth living. The technique usually employs intravenous barbiturate drugs in very high dosage, sometimes accompanied by another drug to stop breathing movements. See chapter 3 for more information.

Intravenous line. A fine tube inserted through the skin into a vein in order to allow intravenous drugs and fluids to be given.

Lasting Power of Attorney. A legal document in England and Wales that appoints one or more people (known as attorneys) to help you make decisions, or to make decisions on your behalf. Lasting Power of Attorneys may deal with health and welfare decisions, or with property and financial affairs. See further discussion in chapter 9.

Liverpool Care Pathway (LCP). An integrated plan introduced in the late 1990s intended to help doctors and nurses within the NHS in England to provide good end-of-life care. There were highly publicized cases in which the LCP was associated with poor care, and an independent review panel in 2013 recommended that the LCP should be withdrawn and replaced by an end-of-life care plan for each patient,

Locked-in syndrome. A rare condition resulting from a stroke at the base of the brain. The person has normal conscious awareness and intelligence, but is almost totally paralysed. The person may be able to communicate by moving the face or eyelids.

Mental Capacity Act. A 2005 Act in England and Wales that covers many aspects of the care of people who can't make some or all decisions for themselves.

Motor neurone disease. A rare neurological condition leading to progressive muscle weakness and paralysis.

Multiple sclerosis. A neurological condition of the brain and spinal cord leading to problems with movement, balance and vision.

Oedema. Swelling and puffiness of the tissues caused by excessive fluid administration or other disease processes.

Opioids. The term for a group of medical drugs that all have a powerful pain-killing effect.

Palliative care. A form of specialized medical and nursing care for patients once it is clear that curative treatment is unlikely to bring any benefit. The primary goal of all palliative treatment is the relief of pain and distressing symptoms, and to help people live as well as possible in the remaining time, rather than the active prolongation of life. The aim is neither intentionally to shorten life nor to try to extend life as long as possible. See further discussion in chapter 9.

Palliative sedation. See 'terminal sedation' below.

Psychotic delusions. A severe mental health disorder leading to abnormal delusional beliefs.

Spina bifida. A congenital disorder of the spine leading to permanent paralysis and sensory problems.

Subcutaneous. Literally 'under the skin'. It is possible to give fluids to a patient through a very fine needle inserted into the soft tissue beneath the skin.

Terminal care (also called end-of-life care). The medical and nursing care given to a person in the final hours of his or her life, a period usually covering a few hours up to two to three days. The aim of terminal care is not to hasten death, but to relieve pain and distressing symptoms, and meet whatever needs the dying person has. See further discussion in chapter 9.

Terminal sedation (or palliative sedation). These terms are used differently in different countries. In the UK and most other countries, it refers to sedation given in the terminal phase of life when the patient is likely to die within a few hours or at most one or two days. The dose of sedative is varied to keep the patient comfortable without compromising respiration or hastening death. In the Netherlands the term 'palliative sedation' is sometimes used to refer to the practice of rendering a patient unconscious with continuous sedation, at the patient's request, for periods of up to one to two weeks without giving hydration, after which death is inevitable. See Appendix 4 for more information.

Further reading and resources

Nigel Biggar, *Aiming to Kill: The Ethics of Suicide and Euthanasia* (Pilgrim, 2004)

Shirley du Boulay, *Cicely Saunders: The Founder of the Modern Hospice Movement*, updated, with additional chapters by Marianne Rankin (SPCK, 2007)

Christian Medical Fellowship and Lawyers' Christian Fellowship, *Facing Serious Illness: Guidance for Christians towards the End of Life* (CMF, 2015)

Ronald Dworkin, *Life's Dominion: An Argument about Abortion and Euthanasia* (HarperCollins, 1995)

Stanley Hauerwas, *Suffering Presence: Theological Reflections on Medicine, the Mentally Handicapped, and the Church* (University of Notre Dame Press, 1986)

Nick Kemp, *'Merciful Release': The History of the British Euthanasia Movement* (Manchester University Press, 2002)

Penney Lewis, *Assisted Dying and Legal Change* (Oxford University Press, 2007)

Gilbert Meilaender, *Bioethics: A Primer for Christians* (Eerdmans, 2005)

Josef Pieper, *Faith, Hope, Love* (Ignatius Press, 1997)

George Pitcher, *A Time to Live: The Case against Euthanasia and Assisted Suicide* (Monarch, 2010)

Robert N. Proctor, *Racial Hygiene: Medicine under the Nazis* (Harvard University Press, 1988)

Fiona Randall and Robin Downie, *The Philosophy of Palliative Care: Critique and Reconstruction* (Oxford University Press, 2006)

Robert G. Twycross, *Introducing Palliative Care* (Radcliffe Medical Press, 2003)

Mary Warnock and Elisabeth Macdonald, *Easeful Death: Is There a Case for Assisted Dying?* (Oxford University Press, 2008)

John Wyatt, *Matters of Life and Death*, 2nd edn (Inter-Varsity Press, 2009)

John Wyatt, *Finishing Line*, DVD and booklet discussions for church groups (CARE / Keswick Ministries, 2015)

also by John Wyatt

Matters of Life & Death

Human dilemmas in the light of the Christian faith
John Wyatt

ISBN: 978-1-84474-367-4
304 pages, large paperback

Rarely are human dilemmas out of the news. And what medical science can do and ought to do – or ought not to do – impinges on our personal lives, families and societies.

John Wyatt examines the issues surrounding the beginning and end of life against the background of current medical-ethical thought. Writing out of a deep conviction that the Bible's view of our humanness points a way forward, he suggests how Christian healthcare professionals, churches and individuals can respond to today's challenges and opportunities.

This volume offers biblical perspectives on humanness, infertility, the quest for the perfect child, genetics, biotechnology and stem cells, abortion and infanticide, euthanasia and assisted suicide, and concludes with a look at the future of humanity. Sensitive and gracious, it acts as a companion to those engaging with the issues in their professional and personal lives, and in public debates.

'John Wyatt's personal integrity shines through this book from beginning to end.' John Stott

Available from your local Christian bookshop or **www.thinkivp.com**